FAMILY THERAPY
IN THE COMMUNITY

For Shona and Gerrie

Life ain't easy,
but it ain't bad.

NEIL DIAMOND

FAMILY THERAPY IN THE COMMUNITY

W. D. MacPhail, RMN

Heinemann Professional Publishing

Heinemann Medical Books
An imprint of Heinemann Professional Publishing Ltd
Halley Court, Jordan Hill, Oxford OX2 8EJ

OXFORD   LONDON   MELBOURNE   AUCKLAND

First published 1988

British Library Cataloguing in Publication Data
MacPhail, W.D.
Family therapy in the community.
1. Welfare work. Family therapy
I. Title
362.8'286

ISBN 0 433 00046 5

Photoset, printed and bound in Great Britain
by Redwood Burn Limited,
Trowbridge, Wiltshire

Contents

Acknowledgements

Many people have helped, directly and indirectly, in the preparation of this book and to them I offer my thanks.

To Martin Vousden for his help in draft preparation and presention, no mean feat.

To Geraldine for the hours of correcting and typing, often done by burning the midnight oil and always in her spare time.

To the staff of the Mental Research Institute for the opportunity to learn together with them and gain experience and confidence in working in family therapy.

To my family for their support and indulgence while their routine was upended at personal cost.

Finally, to those clients whose experiences and problems have helped me gain a better understanding and have enabled me, in turn, to help them. Without them there would be no motivation to struggle to learn better ways of helping.

Introduction

Family therapy has grown substantially since its early days in the 1950s. There are numerous approaches or models of therapy, from psychoanalytical to behavioural, and not a week goes by without the professional press mentioning or featuring an article on therapy. This new wealth of literature is not surprising, considering the growth and original context of family therapy, which developed from individual psychotherapy and was modified and extended for families. Out of this early work came the theories—sets of assumptions which attempt to explain the phenomena presented. As one theory was accepted by some, it was rejected by others who proposed new theories of their own—systemic, structural, strategic, behavioural, interactional or communicational. As these theories were tested to their limits over the last three decades, each school of thought researched and justified its own approach to therapy. In the United Kingdom interest in family therapy increased dramatically in the 1960s when community care began to be implemented. The newness of this concept and the inability of therapists to continue using individual psycho-therapy effectively in family settings stimulated a rush to learn the family therapies which had recently been seen to be effective elsewhere in the world.

This eagerness to learn family therapy continues today in community agencies such as social services, community psychi-atric nursing services, health visiting and, to an extent, district nursing and midwifery. A healthy tendency towards an eclectic approach has developed in proportion to the numbers taking up family therapy as a therapeutic approach. The best, most effec-tive skills have been taken from each school and moulded into an overall approach. This can only be beneficial to both patients or clients and nurses and therapists.

Apart from the socioeconomics of politics which seem des-tined to promote effective community care, it seems a natural progression for the community carer to develop more family-oriented skills rather than individual-oriented ones. This book therefore is designed with these people and these skills in mind. Few of the plethora of available publications seem skill-oriented and fewer designed for the nurse or family worker. It is hoped that this book will provide practical help on *doing* family therapy and not be overly concerned in discussing *why* you should be doing it.

From my experience this book is one which works. This does not mean that others do not, nor that this one always does. The interpretation of theories and techniques is personal and does not exclude the viability of other interpretations. It is also readily recognised that as it is an action rather than a concept book, some of the basic theories, such as systems or psychosocial transition, may have not been properly explained. However, the further reading and references will inform the reader where to find such information.

The words 'illness' and 'problems' are interchangeable in this book: the terms 'patient/client' and 'nurse/therapist' are also interchangeable.

1

The Family

The first rule of family therapy is that there are no rules. That is, no rules can be rigidly defined or adhered to. Family therapy is a concept, based on flexible guidelines. The effectiveness of family therapy is based on individual interpretation of these guidelines in conjunction with the therapist's flair, innovation, experience and perception. Many authors on family therapy have tried to come up with a clear workable definition of a 'family', but find that such definitions are not practical, due to the flexible nature of a family: the family is a concept.

To illustrate this point, Fig. 1.1 shows the three tiers of a family

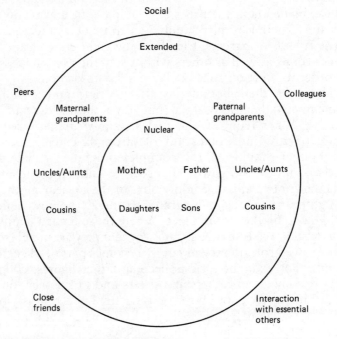

Fig. 1.1 *The three tiers of a family as seen from the child's viewpoint*

as seen from the children's viewpoint. If a generational change is made and the same diagram is seen from, for example, the father's point of view, on the father's side uncles and aunts become brothers and sisters and on the mother's side uncles and aunts become in-laws. Paternal grandparents become mother and father and maternal grandparents become in-laws; cousins become nieces and nephews. It becomes more complex when another generational leap is taken. For example the maternal grandmother has five possible roles: wife, mother, mother-in-law, grandmother and aunt. It soon becomes clear that any individual's familial role becomes more and more complex as each new generation unfolds; in addition, most nuclear and extended families are continually adding new members or losing members. The perception of any person's role alters depending on where he or she fits into either the nuclear or extended family.

This 'jungle' gets even more complex when one includes such human factors as role expectations and emotional and interactional involvement with others. However, it is generally accepted that the nuclear family consists of mother, father and children. The extended family consists of grandparents, uncles, aunts and cousins. There is a third family, which is social and consists of close friends of parents, friends of the children, colleagues and peer groups as well as others with whom interaction is essential in order to function adequately on a day-to-day basis.

However, these boundaries are not rigid and it should be remembered that the essential function of the nuclear family is to survive. When required, the nuclear family can, and frequently does, 'borrow' individuals and roles from the extended family. If the mother should die, for example, an aunt or female grandparent may be borrowed in order to fulfil the vacant role, whether practically or emotionally, of the nuclear mother. If a daughter or son dies, the parents frequently borrow a niece or nephew to fill the vacant place. Where the extended family does not exist, or relations live so far away that they are unable to fulfil a borrowed role, the social family becomes part of the extended family. For example, priests become father figures, colleagues may become like brothers and sisters and I have seen, on some occasions, even paper-boys or girls fulfil the role of sons or daughters. Many factors can and do influence both the perception of the family and the family's perception.

There are also cultural factors which influence the family's attitudes and its methods of functioning. For example, some ethnic minorities seem to place a higher importance on obedience and loyalty within the nuclear and extended families. It could be argued that the concept of the nuclear family in some ethnic cultures includes members of what is normally termed the extended family, that is, grandparents, brothers and sisters and their families. Social factors such as economics, employment, social class, environment and cultural background can add or relieve pressure on the nuclear unit.

These units are more frequently called systems; here we have the nuclear system with its own subsystems. For example, parental subsystem, sibling subsystem, female subsystem (which includes all female members of the nuclear family) and male subsystem. These four subsystems can function individually in their own specific areas while still functioning in the larger nuclear system. The parental subsystem is usually attributed with the power of authority and decision-making while having the responsibility of providing for, protecting and teaching the subsystems. The sibling subsystem on one level provides a two-way emotional exchange while on another, more independent level, is seen to be a play, learning and peer subsystem. The female and male subsystems are most evident educationally, such as the boy who helps his father repair the car or the girl who helps her mother with the cooking. It is during the development of each of these systems that role perception and expectation are formed, usually within the parameters of what society expects and accepts. This means that, in general terms, daughters are expected and encouraged to play with dolls, while boys are expected to play with cars. One can clearly see the perception and expectation of children being directed from an early age by nursery rhymes such as 'Georgie Porgie' or 'What are little boys made of?'

It is also during these formative years that emotional control is encouraged. An example of this is the cultural expectation that boys do not cry, but girls do. Children are also continually taught the moral standards which their parents, society and culture expect of them, such as commitment to others, that helping others is good and that anger, conflict and aggression should be avoided. Obviously, some parents are better at teaching than others and if the child sees different behaviour in the parents to that being propounded, the child will usually follow the example rather than the theory.

As the systems are broadened to include the extended family

and further, the function becomes less specific but usually remains based on loyalty, protection and adequate functioning in day-to-day life. The importance of the basic principles—the family system—functioning and being protected can never be overemphasised. The family maintains a standard of behaviour and interaction which is acceptable to the role-making participants and rewarding to all. These rewards could be anything from financial and material security to acceptance by the peer group or emotional interaction with desired persons (MacPhail, 1983). An example of this is the way that despite family quarrels or arguments, if an external threat appears, the family quickly forgets its own internal disputes and closes ranks in order to fend off the threat. As each system develops and successive systems emerge, their role and function alter to include new information and new experiences. It is therefore clear that family units or systems are essential because of the protection they offer individuals within the system. They also help the individual become a responsible, functioning and participating member of not only his own system, but also the wider system of society. Without initial family teaching, the child has little chance of surviving in society. If he does survive he could have a destructive influence on other members of society.

Although the principles of family systems have remained virtually unchanged since stone-age man, who decided that for economical, political and survival reasons it would be best to form systems or groups, there have been rapid changes in the boundaries and philosophies of the family system. This is especially true since the end of World War II. Immediately after the war there was a rapid change from war industries to peace industries which required the work force to learn new skills as well as accommodate the returning forces. Since then there has been a progressive rapid increase in earning capacity and ways of spending these earnings. Families have consequently become more materialistic, witnessed by the tremendous increase in car sales. This in turn resulted in a much more independent nuclear family. The family now has a method of transport from one end of the country to the other, or, if not, at least the means to afford transport. In contrast, since the financial boom of the 1960s, unemployment has steadily increased while traditional crafts have been in decline. These factors exert a great amount of pressure on the family provider to move around the country to gain employment and financial security. As this occurs, the nuclear family must cut traditional ties with the extended family. As a result, the nuclear family no longer has the same access to the support formerly provided by the extended family. This applies both in terms of protection and in terms of substitution or 'borrowing'. Some would say that cultural pressure and that caused by unemployment on deprived minorities are largely responsible for social phenomena like urban rioting, frequently encountered nowadays. The specific problems of ethnic minorities will be discussed in Chapter 7.

It can be seen that as a result of these changes family resources available to adapt to new circumstances are greatly diminished. This may be one of the factors influencing the increase in referrals to psychiatric services.

There are other types of families which face not only these common problems but also, by nature of their constitution, added pressures. For example, single parent families, dual career families, gay families and mixed ethnic families. Looking back at Fig. 1.1 and the composition of nuclear families, it is easy to understand how single parent families are under extra pressure as they have dual roles—both mother and father—to play. They may or may not be able to 'borrow' from the extended family depending on the family's attitude to single parenting. This is influenced by whether the partner is absent because of divorce or non-marriage. The single parent also has to function in all subsystems where either parent would be expected to become involved; this causes increased pressure.

In dual career families the main problem is one of attitude. If both partners initially agree to a dual career, they can function relatively independently. If, however, one partner decides he or she wants a family, there is an immediate opportunity for conflict and accusations of disloyalty. Another problem for this type of family is that their income will be increased, possibly to the extent that they move or are expected to move to a higher social class. This brings the need or desire radically to alter the social family. It has been suggested that increased independence by married career women is largely responsible for an increase in the incidence of mental illness affecting males (*Sunday Times Magazine*, 1971). This is presumably because of the traditional attitude that man is the provider for materialistic needs while woman is the provider of emotional needs. There may also be conflict and guilt. As both parents pursue their careers, they may feel their children are not being afforded the emotional fulfilment that young children need.

In gay families the pressure tends to result from social attitudes to homosexuality.

When ethnic minorities are involved and the marriage is inter-ethnic or cross-ethnic, the problems will be the attitudes of society and the conflict of differing cultural expectations of the individual's role.

'Normal' family development is as complex and as difficult to define as the family. However, a good baseline is that normal family development is such that the participants of the family system are able to function adequately in day-to-day life and are able to use previous experience or a flexible approach to resolve any new problem which may arise. But if problems arise which cause the system to dysfunction, this can be classed as abnormal family development, irrespective of how transient or temporary the interruption may be. When the family is able to resolve the problem to its own satisfaction, normal development continues.

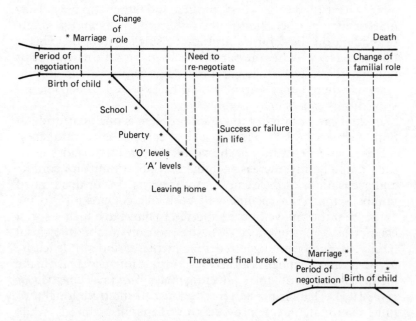

Fig. 1.2   *Life cycle events*

Generally, all families experience the same sort of developmental milestones where the key to continued functioning is adaptability (Fig. 1.2). By definition, the family life cycle is cyclical and consequently never-ending. However, here the family life cycle is taken as starting when 'boy meets girl'.

In the mid or early teens, episodes of courtship tend to be based on purely emotional fulfilment. One of a boy's first actions is to make himself available to girls. This is evident when boys and girls cluster at opposite ends of a room during dances. It is generally accepted that those not dancing are available. The first sense to come into play is vision and comments such as 'She's pretty nice' or 'He's quite good looking' can be overheard. This is usually followed by some form of direct approach, for example by asking 'How about a dance?' At this stage, the most important skill is that of pinpointing a reciprocal attitude. However, if things progress, the olfactory and tactile senses are brought into action and again, if both parties like what they see, smell or touch, the option for progression exists. But if one or other party is not satisfied, the interaction is broken off or actively discouraged so that each may pursue other people. As the relationship develops, cultural, environmental and familial attitudes and values come into play. This is the period of negotiation, when bargaining takes place about the conditions and expectations each has of the other if the relationship is to develop. Now conversation stops being of the 'How many brothers do you have?' or 'What do you do after school?' variety. It turns instead to topics such as 'Do you want to meet up some time and go for a drink?' or 'What does your father do?' This more specific conversation is aimed at finding out detailed information about the other's family system. There may be differences of class, economic capabilities, religion, cultural persuasion or age, which all have to be satisfactorily resolved before any further developments can take place. For example, if a Protestant boy and Catholic girl meet and initially satisfy each other's criteria, the religious differences can be resolved by assessing the rigidity of the other person's attitude to religion. Religion may not be a major factor in itself but when taken in the context of, for example, Northern Ireland, differences may appear to be insurmountable because of the pressure which would be applied by both families. In social or economic terms, it may be that the partner with the higher status is considered 'too posh' for the other. This does not mean that one party or system is right and the other wrong; it simply indicates the underlying principal of the system. When somebody with evidently different system values attempts to intrude into a system, the system closes ranks and defends itself. However, following the initial acceptance by one system of the other, the relationship is ready to develop into serious courtship, which may led to engagement or marriage. So far, the two individuals have been trying to discover whether they are compatible in systemic values and now proceed to discover whether their systems are compatible.

The pre-engagement and engagement negotiations tend to be centred around such things as role expectations and questions of dependence and interdependence. For example, the type of information gleaned at this stage revolves around how financially secure they would be and whether or not they would be able to afford a family. If so, negotiations continue concerning how many children they might have and whether the woman would be expected to give up her career in order to have a family. During this stage unresolved issues from previous negotiations are resolved or compromised; for example, matters of religious conviction, maximum and minimum financial commitments and so on. Sexual compatibility may or may not be explored at this point and may in itself be negotiable. When outstanding differences in attitudes and values have been settled to the satisfaction of both partners, marriage can be the next step. However, this is dependent on continued compatibility because it seems that once the couple have agreed on mutually satisfactory systems 'the quest' is over and there is less need to adapt to others' beliefs and values. This may lead to a slight deterioration in the fulfilment each gets from the other. It is still possible for one system to reject a perceived deterioration in the other person's standards. Should any major area be left un-negotiated it will probably come up again later and, if left unresolved now, will create major conflict in the future. So, here are two people negotiating with each other in an independent way but at any point in the proceedings either has the opportunity to pull out and end the relationship.

Once marriage takes place, there is a subtle change. Instead of two independent systems negotiating, there is a third system—an amalgamation of the two original systems. Once again, it is important not to minimise any problems that occur in early marriage as being a case of 'finding their feet' or 'inevitable ups and downs'. Studies of divorced people have shown that: 'more than one-third believe that the problems which were to lead to divorce had started by the first anniversary of marriage and that by the fifth anniversary the serious difficulties had been present for 73%' (Dominian, 1986).

As the newlyweds become more settled and more familiar with each other's system and the new emerging system, initial difficulties are resolved. This is by negotiation with each other or by consultation with the extended family—the parents and in-laws. Sooner or later the prospect of raising a family, which has previously been negotiated, will arise again. This should bring no problems unless one or other has changed his mind. The conclusion so far is that the need for on-going negotiations on all issues is of prime importance. These negotiations highlight the need for successful family development by flexibility and adaptability.

If a couple decide to start a family, the arrival of a child is one of the most important and traumatic changes which will take place in their lives. There is a dramatic change in the wife or husband role into that of mother or father; the roles of the extended family also alter as parents become grandparents, brothers and sisters become uncles and aunts and the partner's parents change from in-laws to grandparents. It is not easy to change the popular image of parents-in-law (interfering and aggressive people) to that of approachable and benevolent grandparents. It is not surprisingly difficult for some to convince themselves that these descriptions are of the same people. Most people have satisfactory relationships with their in-laws and the popular if untruthful social stereotyping that exists shows the degree of influence which the broad social family can exert on both the extended and nuclear family. In systemic terms, it shows that the smaller the system is, the more liable it is to be influenced by the larger system. No part is greater than the whole.

Not only do perceptions of roles change at this time but practical changes, concerning finance, space and emotional commitment of both extended and nuclear family take place. It is amazing how often new fathers are unable to understand why their wives are unable to give the same emotional and sexual commitment they did before the children were born. The reality of fatherhood differs greatly from people's preconceived ideas in practical and personal terms. Therefore, as with all events in the life cycle, there is a need to be adaptable and flexible to all new situations.

The next major life event which requires adaptability is school attendance. This is because, over a period of five years or so, each individual has settled into his or her new role. When the child begins school things are changed again. For example, the father may wish the mother to return to work for financial reasons but she may want to have more children. Clearly, if there is no satisfactory conclusion to this disagreement, conflict will again ensue.

The next developmental milestone is puberty. This is important as puberty marks the stage when parents stop treating their offspring as children and start treating them as adolescents. If this stage is not handled with delicate understanding, the seeds are sown for emotional problems later in adolescence. Educational qualifications, or lack of them, are significant at this time. Children are told that qualifications are essential if good employment opportunities are to be available; this exerts a lot of pressure on the child to be successful. The implication is that if the child is successful in obtaining academic qualifications, he or she will be able to choose to get a job or continue education, usually away from home. This is the first clear indication to parents that the child will leave home within the next five years or so.

Leaving home is a traumatic experience for both child and parents. For 20 years or so, the parents have been developing interactional patterns of behaviour around the child or children and have heavily emotionally invested in them by protective or providing mechanisms. It is therefore devastating to realise that the secure established patterns of 20 years are to be up-ended and you will soon be returning to a one-to-one relationship with your partner. Because of the multiple levels parents have to function on when there are children, it is understandable that when children leave home parents are astounded to discover how their partner has changed over the years. In addition, it is a natural parental instinct to feel protective towards children and their imminent departure leads to separation anxieties.

It is usually shortly after the child leaves home that any unresolved conflicts of marital and sexual disharmony between the parents emerge. From the parents' point of view it is probably hard enough to re-negotiate the emotional and interactional aspects of the marriage without the added sense of anxiety directed towards the children leaving 'the nest'. As the parents become increasingly anxious in their own re-negotiating role within the context of their anxieties about the children, these worries are transmitted to the children via marital disharmony. The implicit message is that this marital disharmony has resulted from the child leaving home. One could therefore argue that by these mechanics of interaction, the child is being used as a scapegoat and may subsequently develop some form of illness, forcing him or her to return home.

This response has two advantages. First, the parents easily rationalise and postpone their conflict negotiation by convincing themselves that the basic philosophy of any system is to forget your differences when one member is being attacked, in this instance by illness. Thus the parents forget their differences and pull together to protect the child. Second, if the child decides to abort from what was originally seen as positive development—continued successful independence—by a conscious decision the child would probably be held responsible for that act. However, illness is seen as indiscriminate and not controllable. It is believed that if one had the option of being well or ill, one would choose to be well. However, if circumstances dictate that one becomes ill, then circumstances are to blame.

This process is further re-enforced when the child returns home. The conflict negotiation of the marriage roles no longer has to take place as the child is re-involved at home. By his or her presence the child has resolved the marital conflict. Both parents normally thank the child implicitly or explicity, that is: 'Things between us are much better now' or 'Since you've been home, things are better'. Having resolved one (marital) conflict, another soon arises. The child, having poured oil on troubled waters perhaps without consciously knowing how, will soon wish to re-commence independence. As soon as this happens, the entire process is repeated. No new level of functioning has been achieved as a result of the transition or conflict situation, as shown in Fig. 1.3. It is easy to imagine how the child feels about repetition of the process. There is confusion to the point of not knowing which way to turn, what and who to believe. The end result may be a withdrawal from involvement. When verbal involvement is demanded, there may be verbal withdrawal or a totally inappropriate verbal response. As this process is repeated

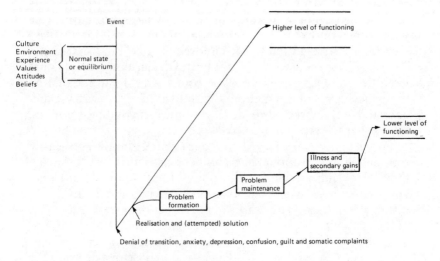

Fig. 1.3 *Psychosocial transition* (PST)

with increasing intensity, the child exhibits increasingly disturbed behaviour and may be labelled 'schizophrenic' by any
person not aware of the precipitating process. This precipitating
process may be denied by the family.

As the young person (no longer a child) goes on to employment
and independence, his success or failure in independent life can
be a trigger, in both his own and his parents' lives, for further
conflict. If he succeeds, either parent may use his success as a
validation of the parent's own decisions. For example, if the
father wishes to move to a smaller house, against the mother's
wishes, he may say: 'When I made the decision about which
college our son should go to, did I or did I not make the correct
decision?' The implicit message is that the father has the ability to
make correct decisions on his own; since the proof of the pudding
is in the eating, his decisions should not be questioned.

The young person may then re-start the entire process at the
point when 'boy meets girl'. It is unfortunate that in the progression through the roles of boy, girl, courtship, marriage,
father, mother, in-laws and grandparents, each role is new and
requires a proportional amount of adaptability and flexibility
because experience was gained only at the previous level and not

at the level of future roles. Throughout this cycle there are times when unpredictable events happen which may throw the system into temporary turmoil, such as a death in the family. When this happens the corresponding nuclear system may need to 'borrow' someone from the extended family, which puts extra pressure on the functioning of the system.

A useful guide in understanding the sequence of adaptability in relation to events is psychosocial transition (PST; Fig. 1.3). Everyone has an equilibrium or normal steady state within which he or she functions. This state includes day-to-day fluctuations of mood. Some days are good and some bad and quite often rapid movement from one to the other is acceptable, as long as it is contained within the boundaries of the normal steady state. The major features of any normal steady state of functioning are cultural standards and beliefs, the present environment and its potential, previous experience and familial beliefs. Each of these components can restrict the level of functioning within the normal steady state and thus, if the equilibrium is unbalanced, would undoubtedly create problems in regaining a functional state.

Taking death as an example of an event, this would evidently disturb the normal state or equilibrium. Cultural factors concerning death obviously differ. The majority of so-called 'advanced' societies see death as a sad loss. Less developed cultures, those relatively untouched by western ideas such as American Indians, see death as the freeing of the soul and a joyful occasion. The environmental factors influencing someone's response to a loved one's death are the amount of support and comfort that could be offered to the bereaved person. However, if the bereaved person has had previous experience of grief, that experience allows him to cope with grief better than someone without that previous experience. Familial beliefs or attitudes, which are akin to cultural ones, usually help prepare an individual to accept bereavement by open discussion of the subject. When death occurs, leaving the individual unbalanced from his normal state, he follows a relatively set pattern of responses which, it must be emphasised, are perfectly normal. Firstly, there is an initial denial of the event. It is quite common for the initial response to be: 'I can't believe it', or 'It's not true. You're lying'. This denial is part of a self-protective response which allows time for gradual adjustment. After denial, there is a general state of confusion during which the affected person questions his own identity and begins to experience anxiety about living without his loved one. This can be related to his own circumstances (within the nuclear family) or circumstances related to those even closer to the lost person (from extended family members). As realisation of the loss occurs, it is generally accompanied by depression which has a component of guilt attached to it. The guilt is twofold. The first part is the 'if only' syndrome in which the person questions his own involvement and, in many respects, tries to deny the inevitability of the transition. For example: 'If only we had not quarrelled'. 'If only we had made up before she left home'. 'If only the other car was going slower'. Second, the bereaved person frequently asks: 'Why me?' This is a response of anger. For example: 'Why did God take my mother when there are plenty of elderly folk living in hospital, not even able to enjoy a good standard of living?' or: 'Of all the cars on the road today, why did it have to be his that was hit?' During this time, appropriate somatic symptoms often accompany the expressed emotion. For example, with expressed anxiety one would expect to see nausea, tension, restlessness and perhaps agitation. With expressed confusion, one would expect to see an inability to complete tasks or follow through specific ideas. With depression, the slowing down of bodily functions and inability to eat fully are observed. With guilt, the 'if only' syndrome appears to generate self-directed anger, whereas the 'why me?' syndrome tends to generate an external anger. All these emotions are culturally and socially acceptable within limits, but in terms of psychosocial transition it can be argued that they are a denial and loss of previous equilibrium. This is a natural response to the loss of a steady state. It is therefore socially acceptable to express these emotions to their varying degrees within the cultural limits of grief and it is defined as a problem or 'illness' if they exceed these limits.

Other events that could alter a normal steady state are taking an examination or a driving test. In the first instance, if the person feels he has performed badly, denial takes place and it is quite common for people to say: 'Well, it didn't really matter; it's not that important'. There is anxiety related to examinations; personally, I can vividly recall the confusion that initially hit me when I first looked at my nursing exam papers.

A similar pattern applies to driving tests. When the events are imminent, the anxiety becomes more apparent. If the candidate fails, guilt is displayed in phrases like: 'If only I'd studied harder'; 'If only I'd read up on the Highway Code'. One can also hear: 'Why did I have to be the only one to fail?' or 'Why did the examiner take it out on me?' There then follows depression or realisation that the actual event has occurred with a degree of loss involved. As with all other guidelines, flexibility and adaptability are essential. Depending on the individual's previous steady state and the type of event which has created the loss, reactions differ greatly from person to person. Some situations create greater anxiety than denial, whereas others create greater denial than confusion. During this period of realisation problems can and frequently do occur. I am deliberately using the word 'problems' rather than 'illness' because problems do not necessarily result in illness, but illnesses do result from mismanaged problems.

If, for any reason, the six components of the normal steady state (culture, environment, experience, values, attitudes and beliefs) are missing or misformed the other members of the family system invoke the protective responses of the system. They recognise that the individual is not functioning as he used to and try to encourage him by saying: 'It's about time you pulled your socks up', or 'It's about time you got back into the swing of things, either socially or at work'. In systemic terms, if for any reason the individual becomes stuck in any part of the sequence of denial, anxiety, confusion, depression and guilt and is unable to function adequately, the system will state that the family member has had enough time to sort himself out and is now expected to function adequately within that system. If this fails, other system members will begin to see the affected member as being ill, as they can only see the emotional or symptomatic responses, that is, denial, anxiety, confusion, depression or guilt. They may therefore call for a doctor. The only problem in involving medical help is that, by implication, the family member is thought to be ill. The doctor may or may not prescribe medication and issue a sick note. These only serve to reinforce other people's perception that the individual is ill. If medical remedies do not work, the patient will remain dysfunctional and may be referred to specialist care, for example, a psychiatrist. Again, by implication, this indicates that the person has a mental illness.

Illness modifies other people's expectations of the ill person, for example, as in the case of a man who had a mild heart attack and after a recuperation period returned to work only to be informed by his employers that if he felt any chest pain he was to inform his superior immediately. He would then be relieved from duty and any existing work load would be spread round his colleagues who would compensate for him. It does not take long for an individual to realise that by implying illness he can reduce the level of his own responsibilities. Another example concerns a phobic patient who has been discouraged from exposing himself to phobic situations, for example: 'I will get your shopping for you', said to an agoraphobic. It soon becomes evident that there are many secondary gains arising from the phobia and, human behaviour being what it is, patterns rapidly set in. In the majority of cases however, such negative processes do not occur and following a realisation of the transition, most people are able to formulate a solution and implement it.

Although these examples concern all major specific times, it is more usual for individuals or families to become stuck at only one of the above points and not several, due to the 'rolling' nature of the family life cycle. This may mean that families or individuals who become stuck at one point may respond in a maladaptive way to that transition and then move on, but at a lower level of functioning, to the next transition. In such cases, the lower level of functioning will be maintained until the next transition or period of need of adaptive responses occurs. As the second transition occurs, the adaptive process is greatly inhibited by the previous negative experience, creating a possible new maladaptive response.

This can be clearly illustrated in what is termed chronic patients, for example, the chronic alcohol abuser who on questioning says: 'It all started 10 years ago when I became redundant and it's been going downhill ever since'. It is clear from this statement that the initial precipitating transition was redundancy but there have been subsequent maladaptive responses to other transitions which have not resolved either the original problem or subsequent ones. Another example would be someone described as follows: 'He first became anxious 12 years ago when his first wife died'. This indicates that the initial transition and current transition are different. Some may argue that the initial reason for the maladaptive response in both examples is part of the current causation of illness. This point is not disputed, but what is in dispute is that since the initial transition the individual's level of functioning has declined and, in relation to the original or previous transition, circumstances and behaviour has changed. It is therefore useful to have these processes in mind when interviewing prospective patients.

Systems theory, life cycle and psychosocial transition are not skills on their own, but they help create an awareness of the process of 'normal' development. They give a clear background from which to observe and pinpoint 'ill' behaviour. They also help to reassure patients that they are not mad but having difficulty managing a difficult situation. How often has the reader heard the plea: 'If only I knew what was happening to me'?

Summary

This chapter studied the generally accepted constitution of families—nuclear, extended and social—and the influences that can be exerted on the nuclear family in terms of family values, support, help and guidance. We have also seen how, over the last 40 years or so, society itself has exerted pressures on the nuclear family both directly and indirectly. The family is under greater pressure today than at any time. From a systems theory viewpoint, the support afforded to any family by extended or social family has decreased for many families. We have also seen how normal development unfolds with relation to the family life cycle and psychosocial transition; this helps us to understand transitions and responses.

Exercises

Ask yourself the following questions and answer as subjectively as possible:

1 What do you think your parents' response would be if you announced that you were to marry somebody from 'a different culture'?
   (Flexible? Traditional beliefs?)
2 Is that response based on assumed knowledge or direct experience of the other culture?
   (What social pressures are there on you to adopt this attitude?)
3 If you are still having problems with your parents on the above subject, how would you go about converting your parents to your point of view?
   (Negotiate.)

4 Which specific emotional or practical attribute makes your favourite aunt or uncle your favourite? Is it an attribute you would normally reserve for your immediate family, that is, mother, father?
(Perception of roles: nuclear and extended do mix.)
5 When you last took an exam or a driving test, did you experience the process set out in psychosocial transition?
(Self-awareness of normality.)
6 Can you think of any other events or transitions on which psychosocial transition applies to you individually?
(Normality.)

It is hoped from these exercises that the reader will appreciate the negotiations that go on within families and with others, and be aware of the pressures he himself may not have to face but others do, and are expected to adapt to in a positive manner. Hopefully, the reader will also realise that when those attributes, usually restricted to members of the nuclear family, are assigned to members outside the nuclear family there is a possible confusion of roles.

Finally, the reader should now have understood the process of adapting to new events and the need to be flexible and adaptable, and be aware of how the process of problems and illnesses begins. It is hoped that the reader can now think: 'There, but for the grace of God go I'. Problems and illnesses are processes to which everyone is exposed; some respond adequately and some do not.

References

Dominian, J. (1986). *Introduction to Marital Problems*. Fount Paperbacks: p. 37.
MacPhail, W. D. (1983). Brief therapy. *Nursing Mirror*; pp. 38–42.
Stag at Bay. *Sunday Times Magazine* (14.3.1971).

2

Families and Nurses

Ever since prehistoric man emerged from the caves and started to form small societies based on self-care, certain individuals within the group were designated to care for those unable to function fully. In other cases, one person was nominated to make decisions about the care of the less able. Thus, there have always been nurses, albeit with the emphasis on curative rather than preventive medicine. It is only relatively recently, that is, during the last 50 years, that nurses have taken their role in preventive medicine seriously and have not acted as the doctor's handmaiden.

It is interesting to note that as early as 1542 the definition of 'to nurse' was 'to promote growth or development' and in 1775 this definition was extended to include 'to assist or cause to develop' (*Shorter English Oxford Dictionary*, 1956). It seems that nurses are still trying to implement these definitions as well as the original 'to care' or 'to look after' (someone who is ill).

In today's climate of general practitioner appointments in which the doctor is only available to assess, diagnose and treat patients within a tight schedule of approximately 15 minutes per patient, it seems self-evident that another health worker (i.e. the community nurse) may be more suited to assess these patients and their problems. Although community nurses have a tight schedule in terms of time available to spend on their clinical case loads, it is more beneficial to spend longer obtaining a clearer, more detailed picture. It is perhaps advantageous and less threatening that the general public tend to see nurses in terms of the more common definition of nursing, that is 'to care' and 'look after' rather than the person who promotes development and change.

As can be seen from Fig. 1.3 (p. 12), as soon as the patient approaches the doctor it is implied that he or she is ill. This process is re-enforced if the doctor issues a sick note or prescription. For rapid resolution it is important to intervene in the illness

19

system as soon as possible, on the principle that, for example, it is easier to stop smoking if you have smoked for only a week than if you have smoked for the last 20 years.

Nurses, midwives, social workers and health visitors have long been accepted as visitors to families in their own homes. This may be the result of being thought to have more time. It may also be that these workers are seen to be less threatening than doctors, who are generally thought of as the bearers of diagnostic bad news, whereas community workers are seen as being there to help. These workers therefore have access to families in trouble on quite a friendly basis. It makes sense therefore that if future programmes of preventive treatment are to be implemented in the patient's home, the best people to do this are those who have already gained access to the home and the family's confidence. However, it would be gross naivety to believe that having gained access, the rest is plain sailing. Many problems must be solved before any form of therapeutic intervention is begun. These can best be categorised as definition ('What do you mean by…?') or anxiety ('But how can I…?').

One of the commonest questions asked is: 'Why family therapy as opposed to individual treatment?' The answer is that in dealing with problems even of an individual nature, the family concept is inescapable. For example, if a mother becomes ill, although she is the person suffering, all members of the family will be affected in some way or another by her non-functioning. Father may have to re-arrange his daily routine and the children will probably be expected to take on extra tasks in order to alleviate the situation. The family system closes ranks, with extra pressure on all members. It makes a lot of sense to use the well members of the family unit to help the ill person regain her functional role as quickly and as effectively as possible. This is not only in her own interests, but also in the interests of the other family members. It is often disregarded that well members of the family usually have a vested interest in the ill person becoming functional again; nurses can provide support and information to this end. I can recall the time I was a patient in hospital and heard nurses tell relatives who were seeking advice on how to support their sick relative: 'You will have to wait and see the doctor' or 'You had better speak to Sister'. Had these questions been of a highly technical nature, one could understand that junior nurses would be unwilling or perhaps unable to offer such advice and refer them to a more experienced member of staff. However, many of the questions the nurses were asked were general enquiries that any member of staff with compassion and a basic knowledge of nursing or surgical procedures would have been able to answer. When I was a student registered mental nurse working on a medical ward there was one occasion when a patient had no visitors. I sat on his bed and tried to discuss his medical problem with him, without giving him information which would be traumatic for him, only to be told by Sister: 'Nurse, you are not allowed to sit on the bed and talk to the patient. Have you nothing better to do?' It is hoped that criticism of nursing staff for being supportive in this context is disappearing.

In terms of family therapy, information given to any members of the family which may help them with the ill person can be deemed to be family therapy. Information given to the relatives will, to a greater or lesser degree, alter their behaviour to the patient or other members of the family. Hopefully the change of behaviour will make the functioning of the family unit smoother and less problematic. Verbal or non-verbal communication directed towards a patient, is, in effect, family therapy.

One issue which arises increasingly is that nurses who have adopted the family therapy approach insist on *all* family members being present at any family interview in the mistaken belief that family therapy must involve all family members. It is more practical and more therapeutically beneficial to see family members who wish to be present, rather than forcing them to be present against their will. It is quite acceptable that some members of the family will be present, some will be absent and som. may actively attempt to undermine whatever is done. There have been occasions when the identified patient has not been seen but the problem has been overcome by interacting with other family members who were willing to help him or her. This will be discussed in greater detail in Chapter 4. There is no therapeutic advantage in insisting that negative undermining forces should be included in treatment strategies, although all nurses should be aware of the existence of these negative forces.

Other practical definitive issues tend to be based on facilities or the lack of them, whether or not the community nurse is clinic- or community-based and peer support. All of these issues can best be covered in a general discussion of perception of role.

As far as facilities are concerned, it is obviously valuable to have video equipment to play back sessions, identify and correct mistakes. However, in the National Health Service we do not live in a Utopian world and therefore have to make the best of whatever facilities are available.

The problems with clinic-based settings are the attendance or non-attendance of clients, over which we have no control, and the motivation factor: if families or individuals do not want to attend, they will not.

The problem with community-based organisations is the time factor involved in travelling from one organisation to the other, plus the work and time involved in setting up video equipment, if available. Where multi-therapist sessions are concerned, it is less economical for a nursing manager to send two or more nurses or therapists on each visit and also more time-consuming. In the light of present NHS economics it seems that the most practical method is to work as an individual therapist. Notwithstanding, cases where multi-therapist sessions or team sessions take place within adequate financial budgets are obviously in a preferential situation.

In team sessions, it is a problem when members of the team are trained to different levels or when some are trained in family therapy approaches and some are not. When members of the team observing behind the two-way mirror cannot follow the train of thought or technique employed by the front therapist (the person directly interviewing the family), they may constantly have to phone through to the therapist and interrupt the questioning to seek clarification. This leads to all kinds of problems in the flow of therapy and the concentration of the front therapist in achieving her goals. Sometimes the family being interviewed become annoyed with the therapists behind the screen, although on most occasions the front therapist can utilise this situation to motivate the patients towards a certain line of intervention. There are intrinsic issues involved here. When all nurses are trained to one level, despite individual experiential progress and understanding within that level, at least all members have common ground, understand and accept the general direction of therapeutic sessions. However, when some members are trained and some are not, the need for clarification is both time-consuming and irritating to the front therapist.

It is interesting to note that those who are not trained in basic family therapy are generally much less liable to use facilities such as video equipment. The untrained members of the team exhibit a perhaps justifiable apprehension of family therapy techniques and skills. I can recall an incident when a nurse not trained in family therapy was asked to help in a session and refused out of anxiety or apprehension and stated: 'Well, it's all imported American rubbish anyway'.

The following issues are those which are subjective and perhaps anxiety-provoking for those who have not been trained in family therapy. These include the nurse's own experience and professionalism in dealing with more than one person at a time. It is relatively common to encounter nurses who feel that in the family therapy setting they would lose control of the behaviours and responses of both the family and themselves. For some reason nurses seem to feel they must be in control at all times when in fact the best advice comes from a nursery rhyme about a wise old owl: 'The less he spoke, the more he heard' (Mulherin, 1981). In order to achieve a therapeutic outcome, it is best to say nothing if you are unsure of the context or the motive for the request for advice. It also seems that nurses are quite willing to accept credit for the success of individual-based therapies but as soon as the family is mentioned, due either to lack of training or of personal confidence, these nurses suddenly shy away. This is despite the fact that each nurse comes from a family and can utilise that experience towards more effective therapy in the community.

Some nurses seem to be unwilling to break with traditional beliefs and branch out into a form of help and caring which entails positive results based on the utilisation of their own experience and skills. An example of this is that many nurses who give or oversee the administration of psychiatric medication cannot reconcile themselves to the fact that medication is deemed to be from the medical model, whereas therapeutic outcome in family therapy can be seen as from the nursing model. There is therefore a conflict of models. It seems that these nurses stick to the traditional belief that the medical model, because of its long-standing implementation, offers greater security both personally and professionally. This in itself leads to personal conflict of interests.

Many nurses state that they are not particularly happy with the family therapy model due to their lack of experience or knowledge in that area. They suggest they would feel much more secure if they could adopt parts of basic family therapy in principle but continue with other models of treatment at the same time. This is a misconception as to jump from one model to another makes the therapist uncertain which model she is using. This can confuse the patients and ultimately the therapist falls between two stools, following neither model effectively. Rationalisations follow such failure: 'Therapy isn't working—it's the fault of behaviourism' or 'Therapy isn't working—it's not my fault—the patient wasn't ready for analysis' (MacPhail, 1983). It is essential that nurses should pursue one model of therapy to the best of their ability rather than try and implement several varying and often conflicting types of therapy.

The problem of peer support is probably the most crucial issue in family therapy, irrespective of model; if the other members of your peer group are not aware of the principles and skills involved in family therapy, they are ill equipped to offer peer support. With the correct form of peer suppport, family therapy can be effective in all settings, whether clinic- or community-based. This of course brings us back to the question: 'Are all members of the team trained in basic family therapy?' Who is the best able of one's peers to provide support? In my experience individual therapists should seek peer support from those they feel closest to professionally, socially and in terms of training experience. There is a long road to travel before standardisations are achieved. At present there are many options available to psychiatric nurses and a vast range of differing models and courses that can be applied for.

One of the greatest stumbling blocks to any progressive model of therapy must be the calibre of the person appointed to the post. It was horrifying to hear a community psychiatric nurse state in relation to the proposed partial shut-down of a 24-hour on-call service: 'Patients do not need support in the hours of darkness'. Such statements reflect the attitudes of the speaker. It does not bode well for any group fighting for professional recognition and status when representatives of that group try to minimise services rather than maximise the therapeutic involvement. Community psychiatric nurses will not be in a position to advance their profession or implement progressive family therapy techniques until standard courses in family therapy and the abstracts of its philosophies are offered and accepted.

This is not a condemnation of the individual nurse but rather

of the system, which allows progressive therapists and traditional nurses to work side by side and expects them to receive
peer support from each other when in fact their intrinsic beliefs
and attitudes are worlds apart. This situation again falls between
two stools: the traditional nurse gains no support from the family
therapist and vice versa.

In the light of line management shake-ups within the NHS over
the last few years, immediate nurse managers are often unable to
fulfil clinical commitments due to their increased administration
and supervisory roles. This may or may not be a good thing, but it
does mean that they are unable to relate closely to the field-
workers in terms of therapeutic strategies and up-to-date knowledge of practice. This may not be the fault of the individual
managers but rather that of the system and is an added obstacle
faced by the novice family therapist. Situations have been known
where the manager of a community psychiatric nursing team
involved in family therapy has been overtaken by his or her
juniors in terms of clinical skills and practical experience. This
raises issues of a practical nature. A manager who is family
therapy-oriented and who finds that his juniors are outstripping
him in knowledge and experience may then cease to take an
active interest in the therapy given by the juniors or even dis-
courage it. This is a natural response in terms of self-protection of
the system.

It may be claimed that such people are in the minority, although I would challenge this. It does seem that this 'minority'
has the majority of say in what the individual nurse or therapist
does. Until nurses are allowed to give of their best in any model or
theoretical field, there will always be this conflict between the
interests of nurses and those of managers or administration. I
have long witnessed the situation where NHS workers have
argued that patients must come first, but in the next breath argue
about their own personal gains from the system. For example:
'We should have greater on-call payments', or 'We should have
higher mileage allowances' etc. I can clearly recall a nursing
officer of mine saying: 'Until nurses stop nit-picking about mileage expenses, the profession of nursing cannot go forward'.

There are of course answers to these problems. There are
courses for community psychiatric nurses run by the English
National Board for those setting out in the community and also
for those who have had some previous experience of working in

the community. These courses go some way towards standard-ising the level of training given to community workers but, in terms of family therapy, there is not yet a basic course of skills, techniques, theories and principles.

However, training and/or knowledge alone do not make the family therapist. The therapist must be able to utilise her own life experiences and adapt or change her own perception of situations. Not least, and perhaps most threatening, a change of perception is required in the ability to leave behind the tra-ditional medical model which very often imparts a sense of security to those who work in it.

An example of how a belief in a system or model can colour one's perception is best exemplified by previous attitudes to and treatments for mental illness. In the Middle Ages it was commonly believed that mental illness was the result of posses-sion by devils. It was therefore appropriate that people from religious sects dealt with the exorcism of the devils. In Victorian times it was commonly believed that mental illness was the result of some criminal element within the personality and it was therefore appropriate for these patients to be dealt with by the penal system, and as a result they were incarcerated. If one embraces the medical model, which until recently was based primarily on the belief that mental illness is a biochemical imbal-ance, it is appropriate that biochemicals, that is, medications, are used as the solution to the problem. These models may be justi-fiable but tend to seek a solution in only one direction. It is unfortunate that they do not allow for the coexistence of other models.

As an example of this exclusivity of approach to mental illness, can the reader visualise being transported back to the Middle Ages? While walking through a village you notice somebody being exorcised or, alternatively, dunked in the village pond. You state that this is totally inappropriate treatment and, according to progressive science, the ingestion of small amounts of poison-ous substances (medication) is the answer for this condition, which is not possession by devils, but an illness which in later years will be called schizophrenia. It is easy to imagine that you, the progressive time traveller, would be locked up yourself or dunked in the village pond for heresy.

Family therapy can coexist with other models of treatment without impinging on their intrinsic tenets. Family therapy is an abstract concept which allows a greater range of options to be available to the therapist in order to promote change and a higher level of coping. It may be that it is because it is abstract that it is difficult to accept and also why some nurses cannot grasp the principles of family therapy. It is not the author's intention to condemn such nurses as there will always be a place for the nurse who cares and helps. However, it could be argued that the place for these nurse is not working with those who wish and are able to promote change or development.

Another possible resolution to the training dilemma is *in situ* training given by the more experienced family therapists within a team to those who have had minimal or no previous family therapy experience. The main drawback here is that an attitude of elitism may be created, for example: 'Who do they think they are, trying to tell us how to do our job?' This brings us back to the ability to change one's perceptions from one model to another.

It seems that what is required is a standardised course on family therapy to be implemented in the current training of community nurses. It would also be beneficial if all members of a particular team could attend any given course, or at the very least, if two members were allowed to attend. Thus the individuals who have been exposed to family therapy skills and techniques have the option of minimal peer support rather than no support at all.

Although the picture presented so far may seem rather bleak and negative, there are many nurses implementing family therapy successfully. The pitfalls and disadvantages outlined may seem sufficient to dampen any adventurous spirit but it would be rare to encounter all of these problems in one setting and unrealistic to ignore them.

For family therapy to become a way of thinking or a way of life, prerequisites and favourable growth are required, much like for a plant. When you want to cultivate a plant, firstly you need the seeds of the plant you wish to grow. Secondly, it would not be appropriate just to throw seeds into the garden and hope they will grow. They need the right soil for promotion of growth and initial protection from the elements. When they are able to withstand the elements, they can then be transplanted into the garden. Due to the special nurturing they have received, they can then survive, bend with the wind and become strong enough not to be uprooted or broken.

So with family therapy, firstly the traditional nurse must have the motivation to adopt a different perception, either because of dissatisfaction with present attitudes or a yearning for knowledge. Subsequently she needs protection from the elements and systems which oppose growth and development; there are two main factions. One is the 'Nothing wrong with traditionalism—it's worked fine for years' camp, who may perhaps be exhibiting a degree of non-adaptability and sense of insecurity in times of change. The other is more subtle in approach, the 'It will never work—it's unethical to manipulate' camp. There is no direct criticism for wishing to try family therapy but an implication that you will be wasting your time. Again there is a hint of anxiety here as, once you are successful, you will be indicating that previous treatments were inappropriate or wrong. Some colleagues have experienced this syndrome with and without the subtlety!

Also required is the right growth-promoting environment. This can best be met by peer support, constructive supervision and adequate basic knowledge, hence the need for a minimum of two nurses per team to attend stimulating and challenging standard courses. These courses must have a practical base with the correct proportion of theoretical and philosophical input. As the seeds take root, protection is still required in the form of supervision by adequately trained and experienced therapists. It is my belief that learning is faster and more therapeutic if you are allowed to make mistakes under supervision rather than by following someone else's guidelines. Under supervision the consequences of mistakes can be minimised, but the learned mistakes leaves an impression. Finally, as confidence and experience grow, so does expertise and, although it may not be ideal, the therapist can now survive with minimum support in even the strongest elements.

It cannot be overemphasised that family therapy is a concept and as all individuals are different, then the implementation of family therapy will be slightly different. The difference between individual-based therapy and family-based therapy is that individual therapy is geared towards changing the behaviour, perception or ability to cope of that individual and not directed at the consideration of the effect on others within the system. Family-based therapy takes into consideration the effect of any change on other members. In many respects family therapy is a greater awareness of the effect of any level of intervention and the skills and techniques used reflect this difference.

Summary

Nurses already have public acceptance to visit families at home. It seems they are the most obvious choice in implementing treatments within the home rather than the previous concept of implementing medical treatment programmes. However, there are many problem areas which need to be overcome prior to treating families effectively. One is the ability of the nurse or therapist to adapt her perception of her role into one which allows greater scope for skills and techniques; she should be aware of the greater range of therapeutic outcomes available. There are many practical difficulties the nurse will face, such as the availability of resources and whether or not they are clinic- or community-based. This chapter looked at the advantages and disadvantages of each; there is little difference between the community- and clinic-based therapist except as regards peer support and practical availability of facilities.

Family therapy skills and techniques are a way of thinking and as such can be adapted to suit firstly the individual patient and secondly the resources available. However, an area of great difficulty is the level of training or expertise afforded to nurses. The author suggests that training programmes should be standardised and, if necessary, separate training programmes should be drawn up for family therapists. If this is not practical, then a standardised portion of current courses available for community nurses should be given over to family therapy skills and techniques. The implementation of family therapy for community nurses is much like Hydra the water-snake; as soon as one problem is resolved, another takes its place. This may be due in part to the essence of the system within which the NHS works, but all systems can be changed. The author can recall a conversation with John Weakland of the Mental Research Institute in California in which he stated: 'There are two ways to change a system: one is to be a rebel, the other to be subversive. The unfortunate thing about the rebel is that he stands underneath his flag, which allows him to be shot at, whereas the subversive can get on with his work and remain relatively anonymous and achieve his goals.'

Exercises

1 How many times a day do you take into account the effect the patient's illness is having on other members of the family?
2 How often have you been approached by relatives of the patient for advice or general information in relation to the illness?
3 Being truthful, how often do you side-step the issue by referring the patient either to your superior or to the doctor?

Questions 1–3 are intended to show that therapy need not be confined purely to the identified patient and that progress in coping can be achieved by advising relatives as well as the patient.

4 Can you recall any situations when you have felt, when asked for a personal or professional opinion, that your response may be too personal or that the family may respond in a way which would be 'out of control'?
5 Have you ever tried talking about your specialist subject (whether within nursing or not) to a colleague for any length of time? If so, what was his or her response?
(This indicates the types of problems in imparting information to another who does not share the same interests.)

Hopefully the reader is now aware of the many problems which family therapists may face and the difficulty in reconciling personal values and attitudes with professional and perhaps medical values and attitudes. In later chapters examples will be given of how to adapt the basic skills and techniques of family therapy into individual situations, as opposed to a panacea type of approach, supposedly covering all eventualities.

References

MacPhail, W. D. (1983). Brief Therapy. *Nursing Mirror*; 157:11:41. London.
Mulherin, J. (ed.) (1981). *Popular Nursery Rhymes*. Granada.
Shorter English Oxford Dictionary, vol. 2. (1956). Oxford University Press: Oxford.

Further Reading

Fisch, R. (1965). Resistance to change in the psychiatric community. *Archives of General Psychiatry*; 13: 359–66.

3

Being Prepared

In order to be prepared, it is essential that the nurse is aware of as many options as possible before initiating any treatment programme. The more options available, the greater the chances of a successful outcome. As stated in Chapter 2, many of the models on offer—exorcism, psychoanalysis, gestalt—tend to preclude the coexistence of other options. However, if one looks at the development and maintenance of problems and how they become symptoms and eventually illnesses, then the options of successful intervention with the individual are greatly expanded. If applied to the individual and family members, the options are limitless. However, this 'quantum jump from original training to family therapy can prove a heady wine for some' (Fisch *et al.*, 1972). It must be realised that wine is not to everybody's taste.

Problems can only occur in situations where mankind has had a direct or indirect influence. That is, problems are man-made and as such, man holds the solution. There is no denying that all individuals and families have problems of varying natures and intensities. However, not all families or individuals are referred to psychiatric agencies for treatment. The key factors which seem to indicate the probability of psychiatric illness evolving from such problems will be studied later in this chapter. It is an accepted observation that: 'in a well functioning family problems may persist but do not paralyse' (Bodin, 1980). Healthy families usually resolve their problems by discussions which may or may not become arguments at some point. The consequence of these discussions is that the matter is settled and the participants enjoy a feeling of being consulted. Therefore the relationship within the system become stronger as a result of positive interaction.

In terms of therapy it is simpler to see the process of problems as three stages. Firstly, problems may occur during a difficult time of adaptation in normal life, as outlined in Fig. 1.2 (p. 6). As previously described, these life events do not in themselves entail problem formation. If, however, problems are mishandled, the participants continue to focus concern on the problems. Secondly, the problem persists as long as concern continues to be focused on the mishandling of adaptation. The problem will also persist by the re-enforcement of interactions of the participants or by others. Thirdly, if this process continues for long enough, maladaptive responses are formed and in order to maintain the status quo of the family or the individual, symptoms of illness or problematic behaviour may then become apparent. This may appear to be a rather simplistic view of problems and problem formation but it should be remembered that the consequence of illness is non-functioning. The ultimate goal of therapy should therefore be to regain a functional level.

There is a plethora of books on the market which explore, discuss and rationalise the underlying 'why?' of illness rather than concentrating on 'what do I do now I am ill?'. An example of this point is the current justifiable concern regarding autoimmune deficiency syndrome (AIDS). It may seem relatively unimportant to an AIDS sufferer where and when AIDS originated or whether the arguments based on moral or religious backgrounds are valid. That is the 'why?'. It seems more probable that the AIDS sufferer would put a higher priority on such questions as 'Is there a cure?' and 'Is the cure available now?' That is the 'how?'. This of course does not diminish the importance of research work undertaken to obtain a cure. However, from the patient's perception, research is of little importance to him until a cure is available.

In psychiatry some patients actually do ask to know the origin of their illness rather than concentrating on achieving resolution of the illness. This may be as a result of the exposure given to certain models of psychiatric treatments and the mistaken belief that if the patient knows why the original 'illness' developed, it would help in day-to-day functioning. I can recall a conversation with a patient on this topic some years ago which went as follows:

PATIENT: The doctor has told me that I need to find out why my childhood relationship with my mother has made me the way I am.
(This patient in her 30s had presented to her doctor with sexual problems within her marriage.)

THERAPIST: Do you believe that the knowledge of the origin of your problems will help you overcome them?

PATIENT: Yes, I am sure it would. The doctor told me that before I can progress, I have to understand what happened with my mother.

THERAPIST: OK. Suppose I found out under hypnosis that the original trauma you had with your mother was that when you were aged three, she ridiculed you in front of all your friends at a birthday party with the result that everybody laughed at you.

PATIENT: But that's not true.

THERAPIST: Just suppose it was true, how would that knowledge help you come to terms with the sexual problems you are having today in your marriage?

PATIENT: Well ... I don't suppose it would help, but it would be interesting just to find out anyway.

This example shows the futility of looking for solutions to current problems in the past, however logical it may seem.

Returning to what would appear to be the intrinsic differences between one family which adapts freely and functionally and another which encounters problems which may lead to problem formation and maintenance, McCorkle and Riskin (1979) published a research progress report indicating seven points which promote healthy functioning in families. These points are:

1 'Healthy families avoid prolonged scapegoating of any one member.' (That is, no particular member of the family is consistently blamed for problems.)
2 'Arguments are quickly followed by friendly interactions.'
3 'Individual differences are respected and encouraged.'
4 'In working on a task, family members co-operate and collaborate rather than bicker.'
5 'A misbehaving child is not allowed to disrupt the family's work on a task.'
6 'Members' comments are acknowledged by other family members.'
7 'Healthy families do not use attributions with negative connotations: a quiet child is seen as shy rather than immature.'

These are of course only indicators which lead to a more

adaptive response in times of problem formation. This may explain why two similar families in terms of social status, financial income etc. can, and often do, respond totally differently to an almost identical problem. Perhaps it should be identified at this point that, in the author's opinion, unresolved problems lead to symptom formation and illness. Therefore, when talking of problems, the author is indicating that problems and illnesses can be one and the same, but that it is more useful and perhaps more therapeutic to escape from the model of 'illness'.

As an example of how fast problems can become symptom-oriented and may progress with appropriate re-enforcement into the bounds of illness, consider a man who has difficulty sleeping one night. He wakes up in the middle of the night. If he is able to recognise that this may occur at any time and to any person and is therefore not a problem, it is unlikely to become one. However, if he becomes concerned that his inability to sleep may reflect on his work performance the following day, he may begin to anticipate problems. He will therefore try to make certain that he can get to sleep and remain asleep the following night. The more he tries to relax in order to fall asleep, the more tense he becomes and thus denies himself the goal, increasing his tension levels. After several nights of this pattern, he may believe he has insomnia and try more extreme methods to counteract his problem. For example, he may stop drinking liquids after a certain time in the evening or he may heat and ventilate his room to a certain level before going to bed. However, this only helps to re-enforce his non-sleeping and as a result, he becomes even more concerned. Before long, concern turns to anxiety which again denies him sleep. Since he is unable to resolve the problem, he will soon look for professional advice. He may go to his general practitioner who may not adequately investigate the problem due to time restrictions on appointments and the man may return from the surgery with night medication. The whole process described above could take as little as two weeks. The unfortunate aspect of this example is that at no point during the process of transformation from a minor problem mishandled to the re-enforcement of illness can this man be described as having acted illogically or irrationally. The conclusion therefore is that logical and rational solutions sometimes do not work. In the context of the above-mentioned man, it is quite possible that his employers and immediate family would express concern about his lack of sleep and his inability to resolve his problem. If this pressure is exerted within the first few days of the problem arising, then even if the man believed his problem would pass naturally without any attempt at intervention, he may be forgiven for bending to the demands of others and eventually seeking medical advice. The man, his family and his colleagues are all responding in interactional terms to his perceived problem with what can only be described as well intentioned, logical and appropriate concern. Unfortunately, however, this does not detract from the fact that their interactional re-enforcement is a negative progression towards illness.

The man's attempt at resolving the situation and his interaction with his family and colleagues are called 'the attempted solution'. The attempted solution does not work as it is, by definition, attempted. The resultant anxiety of non-solution feeds the original fire of anxiety. Sadly, people believe that if a logical, rational solution does not work then it is not the solution that is wrong, but that the individuals concerned are not applying the solution assiduously enough. They will therefore try even harder to use the attempted solution. Clearly this does not work in practical terms. For example, when hammering a nail into a wall, if the nail stops and does not go in to the required depth, the automatic response is to hammer the nail harder.

There are many ways by which people will unintentionally and unwittingly turn difficulties into problems and problems into illnesses. Four of the more common methods are described below. Firstly, the attempt to be spontaneous, a common occurrence in bodily malfunctions, for example, sleeping problems, sexual performance or bowel obsessions. In these areas normal difficulty can be expected at some point, but the individual may define this as abnormal difficulty. He will embark on a particular corrective course, which in turn converts the normal variation in functioning into a problem. An attempted solution is therefore being used to force correction. The individual tries to force himself to sleep, or to perform sexually in whichever way is desired, or to eat special diets or instigate mental guidelines on procedures or times for eating. When this is unsuccessful, he doubles his efforts at the attempted solution, again with no satisfactory resolution. This in turn, re-enforces his viewpoint that his illness must be 'real' and does not respond to non-expert treatments; he then seeks medical help.

Secondly, an individual may look for a safe method of interaction when in fact there are no safe methods. For example, if a shy man wishes to meet a woman but is anxious about his shyness because he fears rejection, he may attempt to summon up sufficient courage to try his luck. However, he will probably interact with the woman in a way which makes him even more self-conscious and blundering to the point where he *is* rejected. If he proceeds further with his line of thought, he will attempt to introduce more aggressive chat-up lines into his opening conversation. I am sure many female readers would admit that a very strong opening line from a male tends to put them off. In this situation there is normally some risk of failure or rejection and yet by attempting to cope in the way described, he increases the risks of failure.

Thirdly, attempting to reach agreement by argument. This is a basis for marital disharmony. Any married person will testify that there are fluctuations in the marital relationship! If such fluctuations are deemed by one or both of the marital partners to represent a deterioration in the relationship, then one partner will probably approach the other with the question: 'What is going wrong with our marriage?' This may be seen as a constructive question but the underlying implication is: 'I think our relationship is deteriorating and I am asking you to discuss it with me as I believe you know the answer and are therefore partially responsible for the deterioration.' If the spouse replies that he or she is unaware of any problem, then the way is open to argument. If, however, the spouse were to reply that there are grounds for believing the relationship is deteriorating, then a less destructive discussion could take place. As most married couples who have such discussions will agree, this situation very rarely leads to relationships becoming closer. Similar situations take place in disagreements between parents and children. For example, if a father is reading the riot act to his son and both retire fuming at the non-conclusion of their argument, mother will probably enter the arena. She may speak to father and son in what is intended as a placatory role but, by making such statements as: 'I am sure he didn't mean what he said', pours petrol on the fire rather than extinguishing it. The implication of the mother's statement is that one should not be angry with the other but as they both are, responsibility and blame lie at their feet.

Finally, focusing attention on oneself by trying to be left alone.

This situation tends to be labelled as 'paranoid' by traditionalists. Normal harassment, encountered daily at home or at work, such as teasing, ignoring or intruding can be seen by some people as an indication of a breakdown in a personal or professional relationship. Once viewed in this way, it is quite justifiable and logical to attempt avoidance of the situation. As these situations occur in conjunction with others, the obvious solution would be to keep oneself to oneself. For example, being unemotional, hostile and indifferent are avoidance behaviours which unfortunately can be and frequently are seen as basic changes in behaviour or personality and may cause offence to others. If this situation is applies to a family setting, then the child who wishes to be left alone and retires to his bedroom will immediately initiate responses of intrusion from his parents, which they perceive as justifiable. The more the parents intrude, the more the child withdraws.

This process is a common psychiatric syndrome known as 'more of the same'. It applies not only to patients' own attempts at pursuing unsuccessful solutions, but also to continuance by the nurse of a particular line of resolution which has already been proven not to work. An example of this syndrome is finding yourself in quicksands. The more you struggle, the more you sink. The more you sink, the more panic-stricken you become and the more you struggle, the more you sink. Thus, problems are maintained by on-going interaction and the interactional patterns may or may not be what caused the symptom to appear originally. Therapy is therefore geared towards 'discovering the governing principles of the family in terms of collective patterns of behaviour of which the symptom is a part' (Sluzki, 1981).

Another area where the importance of the present symptoms is perhaps greater than their origin is in cases of physical trauma, for example, post-stroke depression, post-natal depression and sexual abuse. This is not to say that in these cases the originating circumstances can be discounted, but that attention should be focussed on the context of the presenting symptom rather than the original situation. For example, during a workshop, a member of the audience recounted that following a horrific car crash several years before, she had been unable to sit comfortably in a car as a passenger without experiencing high levels of anxiety. She was, however, able to be a composed passenger if her father was driving or her brother, who had been the driver in the car crash.

She was set some simple tasks to do that evening and asked to report back the next day. She later informed the workshop that she was much less anxious as a passenger, but she could not understand why more emphasis was not placed on finding out more about the original accident. It was pointed out that insight is not a prerequisite to development.

Problems and symptoms therefore rapidly become illnesses due to the rigidity of, or lack of adaptability of, the participating members in that system. Problems can be categorised into three groups:

1 Cases where the problem is being mishandled, described above.
2 Cases where a behaviour, symptom or interaction is required to stop. (For example, when parents request a son to stop aggressive behaviour, or, more subtly, when the parents of a schizophrenic man request that he ceases to display symptoms which are distressing to them.)
3 Cases where a behaviour or interaction is required to start. (For example, parents request a child to start re-attending school, to start obtaining school grades which they believe are appropriate to his potential. Or the manic–depressive is requested to start behaving in such a way as not to cause disruption to colleagues.)

With the understanding and acceptance of this process, it becomes simpler for the nurse to intervene successfully. A wide variety of options are available to the nurse to gain these objectives.

Returning briefly to beliefs in a particular model and how this affects perception, it is amazing that because the mind is thought of as a complex, intricate entity, problems related to the mind must have complex, intricate solutions. I have often mused over a crossword puzzle and imagined complex games ravelled in a clue, only to find the following day that the answer was relatively simple. Such are the mechanics of problem formation, problem maintenance, symptoms and illness. Bearing in mind the belief systems, perceptions, attitudes and values patients and professions have in relation to illness, it makes the nurse's life a lot easier if she adopts this non-abstract approach and uses it at all times.

There are, of course, various methods of referral; verbal, written or direct. There are also many agencies from which referrals are accepted by the community worker, for example, district nurses, health visitors, doctors, consultant psychiatrists, registrars, general hospital medical staff, general hospital nursing staff, social workers, probation officers, police, direct referral by the patient and various voluntary non-statutory organisations within the community. The methods of referral and the constraints on referral agencies are usually specified by district health authority policy or by the individual team's policy and procedure. Some teams can only accept referrals from consultant psychiatrists, others from psychiatric medical staff. At the other end of the range, some accept referrals on a virtual 'open door' policy. That is, anybody can refer himself with, or on occasions without, consent from the general practitioner. Teams which accept referrals without general practitioner consent usually have a medical officer *in situ* willing to take legal responsibility for prescription and treatment regimens. Although the above-mentioned referral agencies come under the system of community workers, they obviously have a definitive special area of interest in the care of the patient. It is important that this should be clearly understood; each agency is biased in its request for a referral from its own specialty. For example, information given by a health visitor referring a mother to community psychiatry will tend to be more biased toward the effect of the mother's illness on the development of the children. The consultant psychiatrist will be more biased toward the medical model of biochemical imbalance and the implementation of medical model type treatments. The district nurses will be more biased toward the psychological effect of physical illness on the patient. Police will be more biased on the criminality aspect of responsibility and the social worker on the more practical social implications of illness. Visualise a patient suffering from depression being visited by each of the above agencies. If that patient is referred to community psychiatry by all of these agencies, although the basic factual information on each referral would be the same, it is not hard to imagine that the descriptive part of the referral would vary greatly. It is highly probable that there would be five different definitions, five different implications and five different methods of dealing with the problem. The unfortunate part is that they are all right in terms of their own perception, and this may create problems on receipt of the referral. As each referral is based in the common language of the referral agency, it is obviously also based on that type or model of perception. If you accept, without question, the perception of the referral agency, it is more likely that you will see the patient within that perceptual model. For example, if the referral letter states that the patient is schizophrenic and you accept that perception, your visit will be based on looking for confirmation or denial of the existence of schizophrenia in the behaviours of the patient, and similarly with any other diagnostic category included in the referral letter. Bearing in mind that your perception may now be free of the implications inherent in each model, it would then be unfortunate to see a patient while subtly adopting one of these models.

Fig. 3.1 shows a referral data sheet which is relatively uncluttered by the common descriptive biases used by varying referral agencies. It is preferable for these forms to be used directly by the referring agency rather than for information to be transferred on to them from a referral letter. For obvious reasons the identified patient's name and address are essential. In teams where there is a geographical division of patches, it is helpful to have the name of the community psychiatric nurse as, if nothing else, the referral agency can associate a particular nurse with a particular area. Where there is no geographical allocation of patches, then the nurse manager can insert the name of the nurse to whom the case is allocated. The age and date of birth are also helpful in indicating the possible types of problems the family may be encountering in terms of life cycle events. This, together with the description of problem, presents the type of scenario the nurse may face. Telephone number is useful as, in some instances, described later, it may be preferable to make contact with the individual or the family before visiting. The name of the general practitioner is essential in teams where there are no *in situ* medical officers as the GP is responsible for treatment administered—including nursing treatments—to patients living in the community. It is also useful to know who the referrer is in that it may be a different agency from the GP and this information may be used for statistical analysis of where referrals come from. (If the referrer is different to the GP, then it should be remembered that the GP should receive copies of the initial assessment reports (Fig. 3.2; see p. 48) and copies of summarised progress reports throughout the duration of treatment.) The family source of

Referral Data Sheet

Community psychiatric nurse ....

Name .... Age/DoB ....

Address ....

....

....

Telephone number ....

General practitioner ....

Referrer ....

Family source of contact ....

Description of problem (in interactional/communicational terms)

....

....

....

Referrer's signature ....

Agency stamp/address ....

....

....

Has the general practitioner given consent to this referral? YES/NO

Fig. 3.1 *Referral data sheet*

contact is one of the most essential pieces of information that can be gathered before visiting. This indicates which member of the family system approached the referring agency with a view to obtaining help. It is quite possible that all the names on the form will be different, although one or two may be the same. In this case, a slightly different approach may be required. The description of the problem is specifically designed to be either interactional or communicational in language. This minimises the input of biased perception, since professional jargon is not acceptable as an interactional description. This excludes diagnostic categories, for example, schizophrenic, schizoaffective, manic–depressive, neurotic, anxious, depressive etc. Of course, the form is only as good as those who complete it and there is no doubt that some agencies will continue to use their 'jargonese' terms. However, perhaps this method of requesting a description is a subtle means of attempting to get other agencies to look at their own perceptions. Finally, the requirement of the referrer's signature is essential. As nurses we do not have the power to initiate and implement treatment programmes without some form of medical authority or cover, whether actual or implied.

Having considered the contents of this form and that of other types of referral forms, it seems that any other information is superfluous as it does not indicate what is happening today but refers back to the previous history of the patient. Although previous history is interesting and may be analytically fascinating, it does not serve much purpose in establishing the best possible method of intervention in current problems. Like reference books, the past history is useful to dip into on occasions for cross-reference, but is not of much practical value when attempting to assess the best direction to take with an individual. If any important information can be gleaned from the past, it would be better if it was gleaned first-hand rather than second-, third- or even fourth-hand. If it is deemed important enough by the patient, he will inform the nurse himself during the initial interview.

Patients can be referred to therapy for three main reasons: firstly, they wish help for themselves; secondly, someone else (usually a family member) seeks help for them, or thirdly, they have been told to seek help under ultimatum or threat. Those who come into the third category will be discussed in greater detail in Chapter 6 as patients referred under duress, and the techniques used to involve them in therapy will also be explored. The referral data sheet differentiates between these points and this information is therefore to hand prior to visiting.

The three main types of patients are best described in an analogy used by the Mental Research Institute. Firstly, there is the customer who goes into a shop knowing roughly what he wants to buy. To a large extent the salesperson only has to inform him whether or not that product is in stock. Secondly, there is the customer who goes into a shop knowing he wants a product, but unsure of the merits of any particular make or model. It is then the salesperson's pitch to inform him of the advantages of each model and help him choose. Thirdly, there is the customer who enters the shop simply because it is raining. This customer behaves as if he wishes to buy something but actually has no intention of doing so. This customer cannot be convinced that it is essential to make a purchase.

The first type of patient knows that something is wrong and perhaps has a rough idea what. He can identify the problem area and perhaps even the mechanics of the problem. In general terms this patient can be treated quickly and effectively using minimum skills as he knows roughly what he wants and what is acceptable to him. In the second type of patient, it is possible that the identified patient is either unwilling to enter therapy or may be unaware that therapy has been requested—this information can be gathered before the initial assessment. Therapy need not be a lengthy process if the nurse has sufficient skills and techniques at her disposal. The third type of patient uses up therapy time and creates an atmosphere of frustration and sometimes overt anger and aggression. The patient who does not wish 'to buy' should be informed of the futility of entering therapy at this point and requested to return when his motivation is greater (see Chapter 6). Unsuccessful attempts to persuade this patient to enter therapy with a constructive, positive attitude often wear down the nurse's patience and commitment. Due to frustration it is quite common for the nurse to refer the patient to another agency or another nurse. The patient rationalises termination of therapy as follows: he has entered treatment and been co-operative but has not been helped by the unrealistic tasks or advice given by the nurse. This process quickly produces what is commonly termed 'the professional patient'.

There is no reason why information-gathering cannot take place at the earliest point of contact, whether face-to-face or by telephone. If the patient is not on the telephone or it is too time-consuming to enter into correspondence prior to visiting, then a confident nurse can proceed on an initial visit with the relevant information gathered from the referral data sheet. As noted earlier, the first type of patient presents minimal problems in terms of pre-referral contact. However, the second type of patient (third-party request) can present with various problems which it is best to clarify before visiting, that is, whether or not the identified patient has for some reason passed his request for help to the third party or whether the third party is requesting help for himself or the identified patient. This can best be exemplified by the following standard telephone conversation:

NURSE: Mrs James, Dr A has asked me to call round to see your husband. I was wondering when would be the best time to call.

MRS JAMES: How about Tuesday morning?

NURSE: Tuesday morning would be fine. How about 10 o'clock? By the way, could you possibly tell me the kind of problems you or your husband are having? It would help me to be better prepared when I visit on Tuesday.

MRS JAMES: 10 o'clock is fine with me. My husband asked me to see the doctor for him because he is feeling so depressed lately.

However, in some instances the last response may read somewhat differently:

MRS JAMES: Well, in actual fact, my husband doesn't really know that somebody is coming. He knows I went to the doctor but he thinks it was something to do with me. I'm having a terrible time with him as I can't get him to do anything and I am getting very upset and run down by continually having to look after him.

This kind of statement may have the added rider of:

MRS JAMES: Please don't mention to him that you come from psychiatry as this would make him even more upset.

As can be imagined from the information elicited from this very simple, short telephone conversation, the response received when visiting such a patient without making pre-visit contact could vary. For example:

MRS JAMES: Come in. How nice to see you.

or:

MRS JAMES: Mr James doesn't know you're a psychiatric nurse so could you modify your approach accordingly?

Or, being ignorant of this fact and announcing yourself to Mr James only to receive the response:

MR JAMES: My God! Who said I'm mad? I'm not mad. I don't want to see you.

The consequences of this last conversation would cause hostility in the relationship between Mr and Mrs James and may initiate hostility from Mrs James towards the nurse for being insensitive. Where the identified patient is either unaware that you will be calling or unaware of your title, then in order to avoid the kind of problems outlined, it is best if the nurse seeks to see the family source of contact—in the above case Mrs James—on her own initially. This can best be justified as:

NURSE: I want to get a clearer picture of the kinds of problems you have.

and/or:

NURSE: I don't want to upset Mr James on our very first meeting.

This fits in with the picture presented, as Mr James apparently does not know he has a problem or is creating a problem, or may even be denying the fact that a problem exists. However, Mrs James has obviously identified the problem and by initiating contact and seeking help is indicating her willingness to get things changed in order to make her own life easier. Either way, a disastrous confrontation has been avoided and the willing party within the system is now aware that the nurse wants to help. Hopefully these examples indicate that it is better to spend a little time avoiding problems rather than trying to deal with them when they arise. These examples illustrate how best to start on the right foot and as a result make life easier for the family concerned and also the nurse.

Having cleared the way by eliminating unnecessary information and concentrating on clear and relatively objective facts, the path now seems clear to commence the initial visit. The format of the nursing team's assessment form in itself indicates their attitude toward and perception of illness. It is therefore helpful if the assessment form which is sent to the referring agency and/or GP, consultant psychiatrist or other agencies is minimised to include only clear, objective information. Fig. 3.2 illustrates a comprehensive collation of essential information without being overloaded with descriptive jargonistic categories. The top half of Fig. 3.2a shows factual data, similar to the referral data sheet, but in addition it identifies the address, telephone number and name of the service responsible for issuing the assessment form. Also featured here are essential internal data required for administration purposes. These include the allocated file number and whether the referral is primary, i.e. no previous psychiatric history known; secondary, i.e. if previous psychiatric history is known and whether the previous involvement was with that service; professional assistance, i.e. when a request has been made by another professional agency for a one-off assessment which will not require follow-up visits by the community psychiatric nursing service, or re-referral, when the patient is already known to that particular service and, following previous involvement, has been discharged and now re-referred.

One other category not listed on the referral data sheet is unit/system members. This is designed to clarify which members of the family live in the same house and therefore have a vested interest in the outcome of therapy. This includes transient members such as visiting sons, daughters or parents who, although not living in the house, may have an interest in the outcome of therapy.

The bottom half of Fig. 3.2a is aimed at amalgamating the varying perceptions of the family members and the identified patient together with those of the nurse, against a background of relevant physical and psychiatric history and in relation to how that history affects current problems. The statements inserted by the nurse under current problems should be as concise as possible, not include too many descriptive terms but rather interactional or communicational terms. For example, the patient may see the problem as: 'I am schizophrenic'. This is a descriptive statement and can mean a multitude of things to a multitude of people. It is much better to ask the patient to define in interactional terms what this means. The need for clarity also applies to other system members and the nurse. This form can be used by the nurse as a self-assessment of her objectivity and non-description.

(a)

Assessment Form

Community psychiatric nursing service

Office address   File number   Primary
Telephone number   Secondary
                                                     Professional assistance
                                                     Re-referral

Date: Referrer:

Name: DoB:

Address:

Telephone number:

General practitioner :

Unit/system members :

Reasons for referral request:

_____

Relevant physical and psychiatric history:

Current problems:
Client

Other system members:

Therapist:

Fig. 3.2   *Assessment form. (a) Factual data*

(b)

Assessment Form

Assessment of current situation:

Management strategy:

Goals to be achieved:

Estimated time span for treatment:

(b) analysis of current situation and goals to be achieved

In Fig. 3.2b, assessment of current situation is intended to elicit a definition of the current situation in interactional terms. This is followed by management strategy, a brief outline of the intended therapy and how it should help. Goals to be achieved and esti-mated time span for treatment are included in order to help the nurse have a realistic outlook and also to remind her that if the desired goals are not reached within the allocated time span, then a re-assessment must take place. The re-assessment should be by another nurse as it is much more therapeutic for both the patient and nurse-therapist if she can say: 'Why isn't it working? I must be doing something wrong', rather than looking at the patient forlornly, implying: 'Why aren't you getting better?' Failure to achieve goals is frequently passed on to the patient as concrete evidence of his lack of motivation rather than stating: 'I am not selling this willing customer the goods,' to revert to the analogy of the salesperson. As indicated, this is purely a provisional form that the author believes would be beneficial; it is up to the individual nurse or team of nurses to implement and adapt their own forms.

Now that the tools for doing the job have been identified, there is nothing to prevent the job from being done.

Summary

This chapter has looked at the normal process of problem forma-tion and the transition from problem maintenance to symptoms and illness. These origins of illness may appear insignificant in genesis but do not acorns grow into one of the strongest of the trees? The interactions around the symptom-bearer have also been noted in terms of promoting the symptom in some situ-ations. Thus, there is the need for a family-oriented approach. This chapter also included a brief look at some of the points which seem to differentiate between coping and non-coping families, and which will help to distinguish between transient problems and long-standing ones.

The various methods of referral and types of referring agencies were outlined, as well as the inherent tendency of agencies (nurs-ing included) to use 'jargonese'. In terms of therapy this is seen as being non-functional usage of language and may bias the nurse's perception towards looking for symptoms and interactions which are superfluous and at times negative to the therapeutic aims of treatment. The need for objective, factual information before referral was outlined as well as the continued need to surround yourself with tools which are conducive to helping you remain objective and factual. Illustrations were given on how to obtain this information, thus avoiding confrontational issues at the outset.

Exercises

1 Try to identify what the family or significant others are doing which keeps the patient ill. (Identify the attempted solution.)
2 How many of the seven indicators of a healthy family can you see in the families you visit?
3 Can you identify examples of the 'more of the same' syndrome?
4 Which of the three groups do your referrals fall into? (That is, something is required to stop or to start or is mishandled.)
5 Look at present referrals and see how many are model-oriented in presentation.
6 In your present referrals, who is looking for therapy on behalf of whom?

These exercises will help you to question the information you receive and assist in cataloguing that information objectively in your mind. They will help you be objective when visiting patients without having to make a conscious effort other than ensuring you do not follow or accept descriptive language.

References

Bodin, A. (1980). The interactional view: family therapy approaches of the Mental Research Institute. In: Gurman, A. S., Kriskern, D. (eds.), *The Handbook of Family Therapy*. New York, Brunel/Mazel, p. 274.

Fisch, R., Watzlawick, P., Weakland, J., Bodin, A. (1972). On unbecoming family therapists. In: Ferber, A., Mendelson, M., Napier, A. (eds.), *The Book of Family Therapy*, New York, Science House, p. 598.

McCorkle, M., Riskin, J. (1979). Nontherapy family research and change in families: a brief clinical research communication. *Family Process*; 18: 161–2.

Sluzki, C. (1981). Process of symptom production and patterns of symptom production. *Journal of Marital and Family Therapy*, pp. 273–80

Further Reading

Watzlawick, P., Weakland, J., Fisch, R. (1974). *Change: Principles of Problem Formation and Problem Resolution*. New York, W. W. Norton.

4

The Initial Interview

Many skills and techniques in family therapy enable and enhance the therapeutic outcome. Most of them are logical and natural and the reader may experience the fleeting thought: 'I already do that'. But by definition of the word skill, if it is being performed unconsciously, it cannot be a skill. Skill is generally defined as 'an ability which is constantly practised until a level of expertise exists' (MacPhail, 1986).

Unfortunately, the first skill which must be mentioned and is especially relevant for community nurses is that of courtesy, that is, politeness and consideration for others. Some nurses seem to think they are in a more powerful position than their patients and need not be polite or considerate to them. The author has heard of several instances where a community psychiatric nurse was physically thrown out of a patient's home. It later transpired that this was because the nurse had been extremely discourteous and unduly aggressive toward the patient. Treatment is based on verbal exchange. The patient will verbally inform the nurse of his perception of the problem and the nurse will then verbally inform the patient of the best way to approach that particular problem, in her professional opinion. It is appropriate that consideration and politeness should be extended to the patient and his perception of the problem, whether or not that perception is correct, incorrect, excusable or inexcusable in the nurse's opinion. Any functional person would be indignant if a relative stranger came into his home and stated that his perceptions were rubbish or of no consequence. This situation is greatly aggravated when the person happens to be non-functional and perhaps has the added stresses of inadequacy, guilt, anxiety or possible hardship to bear.

After the skill of courtesy comes the more professional courtesy of confidentiality. On trains, buses and in public houses, nurses openly discuss intimate details of patients in their care with each other and with non-professional friends. The following conversation was heard recently in a public house:

MS A: Did you know that old Mrs Smith down the road was admitted to ward 6 this week?
MS B: No, I didn't. What a shame. She seems a dear old lady.
MS A: Dear old lady! She's nothing but a sodding, filthy cow.

This conversation went on to describe Mrs Smith's behaviour and it appeared that she was doubly incontinent and somewhat confused. When these two nurses were confronted on the issue of confidentiality, they reminded me that I should not be eavesdropping and it was none of my business anyway. Such incidents do occur, perhaps rarely, but nonetheless, they do occur. I am sure that if NHS staff were admitted to hospital as patients, they would not feel very comfortable knowing that their intimate personal details might be discussed in a public forum. It must always be remembered that the nurse is in the patient's house by invitation and it is a gross insult to abuse that privilege.

Appropriate appearance should also be included as courtesy. Some nurses, wishing to blend in with the community they serve, seem to believe that the majority of the population dresses in sweaters, jeans and sneakers. This does not mean that nurses should wear designer dresses or pin-stripe suits but, with a little effort, nurses can remain comfortable and presentable to all ranges of patients. Human behaviour is such that first impressions are lasting impressions.

The initial interview is extremely important as it sets the baseline for subsequent interviews and is the first of various inter-related steps of treatment. The first step is the most important and must be in the right direction. As the author was once told by his father: 'If you want to head west, but are facing the north, you will never get there'.

The aims of the first interview should be to find out sufficient clear, specific information on the nature of the presenting problem, how the problem is being handled by the client and family members and the goals of treatment as seen by the client and family. However, it is possible that when you arrive, the identified client will not be available or perhaps the person who requested help from your referral source will not be available. You may be frustrated but the format for the initial interview can be utilised with whoever is present. It just means that you approach the problem from a slightly different angle, bearing in mind that all members of the family are probably affected by the identified client's problem.

As to the question of how to identify yourself on the doorstep, the author finds the most therapeutic and least confrontational way is simply to state: 'I am (name) and (referrer or referral agency) has asked me to call round to see if I can help you with the problem.' This leaves the therapist's options open as the identified client or relatives may not have been informed that a member of a psychiatric service has been asked to visit by the referral agency.

In order to avoid the previously mentioned power position, it is often best to adopt what is termed the 'one-down' position, as opposed to the 'one-up' position which indicates power and superiority. The problem with the one-up position is that by implication you are deemed to be an expert and as such, due to your vast knowledge and experience you should have answers to all problems. This may generate an inner warmth but also means that the client and family will expect you as an expert to give an immediate solution to their problem. Unfortunately therapy is not that simple. As a reminder of the definition of nursing, as described in Chapter 2, the role of treatment should be to promote growth or development. That is, the individual and family should do the majority of the work, albeit under the discreet guidance of the therapist. The best way of adopting a one-down position is to introduce yourself initially by your Christian name and surname. Then ask each individual if you have his permission to call him by his Christian name. On that basis, they can use your Christian name. This reduces the formality so often found in power situations. It also presents the therapist as humanistic and caring.

This brings us to the information gathering, remembering that the therapist also has an assessment form (Fig. 3.2; p. 48) to complete. It is often best to follow the format of the form. Most of the information required in the top half of Fig. 3.2a can be completed before the visit. The overall subject of the therapist's administrative responsibilities can best be broached to the client and family by stating something along the lines of: 'Would it be all right if I just get some details before we actually start?' Then proceed to ask who are the residing family members and who are visiting family members and if possible, how frequently they visit. As far as primary and secondary categories are concerned, the simple question: 'Have you ever been seen by anyone in psychiatry or psychology before?' is sufficient and will give you the appropriate category. In the case of a re-referral, it is suggested that the therapist checks any index cards in her office. If the client has a previous history, this will be apparent from the index card and the question need not necessarily be asked. It is also relevant at this point to state that any previous involvement is important as this may indicate previous attempted solutions which presumably have not worked. As a way of reducing the client's possible fears and anxieties in relation to records and administration, it may be pertinent to ask if it would be all right to take notes: 'I can't remember everything and I don't want to miss anything that may be important.' This allays the client's fears that he is dictating to the therapist and also re-enforces the one-down position. It is suggested that this procedure should be employed whether or not the therapist has a good memory.

The next part of the procedure is to get a clear, precise definition of the problem from the point of view of the client and other family members so that the therapist can make an objective assessment of the interactions and behaviours surrounding the problem. To do this the therapist can ask the simple question: 'What's the problem?' This should be followed by asking other family members present: 'How do you see it? How does it affect you?' It may be that all family members will respond with similar statements. But it may be that one family member will give a diagnostic response and others practical responses in terms of the consequences of the diagnosis. For example:

FATHER: I feel so depressed I want to end it all.

THERAPIST TO MOTHER: How do you see the problem and how does it actually affect you?

MOTHER: Well, I know he's depressed but that doesn't really help me because I've got to take time off work which means I'm losing money. We're just about at the end of our savings.

THERAPIST TO SON: How does all this affect you?

SON: It means I can never do anything right. It means that I've got to stay in and look after Dad.

As can be seen from this brief conversation, although there

may only be one problem, there are three perceptions, not just of the problem but of the consequences of the ensuing interactions to each individual. It is therefore necessary, in the above example, when talking to Mother to remember that although she is sympathetic toward the identified client, her motivation to overcome the problem is financial. The son's motivation for resolving Father's problem is in terms of his own freedom or independence. It is important that the therapist should use their motivation as a basis when she discusses what she would like each of these people to do to help resolve the situation.

At this point two skills come into use: the empathic response and concretisation. The empathic response is the ability to judge how another person might feel in his situation. This may be drawn from the therapist's previous personal experience or at least should be based on common sense. If the therapist employs the empathic response, not only does she bridge the emotional gap between herself and the client but she also re-enforces the one-down position: 'I've been there too. I am human.' An example of the empathic response is:

CLIENT: I am really upset because last week my dog died and as if that wasn't bad enough, this week my sister was killed.
THERAPIST: That's terrible. I know just how you feel. My dog died recently and although I don't have a sister, I can remember how I felt when my mother died.

The important point is that this statement must be based on fact and not made for effect. If the therapist does not have previous experience of this nature, then a more appropriate response would be:

THERAPIST: I think I know how I would feel if I were in your shoes. It must be terrible to lose somebody so close.

Concretisation is the skill of not accepting abstracts, such as feelings or adjectival statements (descriptive), as being fact. Such statements are the result of practical, concrete interactions and not the cause of them. Concretisation means getting the client to describe the problem in terms of observable behaviour, i.e. what can be seen and heard. Although statements related to a person's emotional perception are useful, they are not very important on their own. But in conjunction with the behavioural description, they portray the client's attitudes and values. In terms of perception, reliable information need not necessarily be 'the real truth' but should be a clear account of the interactional situation from that person's point of view, a perception which says: 'This is how I saw it' and is hopefully sufficiently clear and specific so that the therapist can obtain a reliable idea of how things would have been if she had witnessed the situation first-hand. The best explanation is for the therapist to imagine that the participants of the problem each have a video camera on their shoulders. By questioning in such a manner the therapist can omit the personal biases of the participants. For example:

FATHER: It doesn't help me when she (Mother) blames me for everything.
  (Descriptive statement.)
THERAPIST: How does she blame you?
  (Request for concrete information.)
FATHER: I just know she does by the way she looks.
  (Supposition.)
THERAPIST: Could you give me an example of what she said or did that makes you think she blames you?
  (Request for concrete interactions on which the previous supposition is based.)

The client is asked to provide concrete evidence which supports his perception or he must state that he does not know why he has made such suppositions. Either way, the therapist can eliminate the client's possible negative influences of perception. An example of how easy it is to be drawn into the realm of abstracts is as follows:

THERAPIST: What's the problem?
CLIENT: I feel depressed.
THERAPIST: How depressed do you feel?
CLIENT: I feel very, very low. I feel as if it's not worthwhile.
THERAPIST: That must be terrible.
CLIENT: It is.

This conversation has now come to its logical limit and, rather than create a conversational hiatus, the therapist would probably leave that theme and branch off at a slightly different angle. However, if the therapist had followed the concretisation method then the options would still remain open. For example:

CLIENT: I feel depressed.

THERAPIST: That can't be very nice. Could you possibly tell me how it affects you?

CLIENT: Well, I just don't seem to want to get out of my bed.

THERAPIST: What are the implications or consequences of staying in bed for you? Does it mean you cannot go to work? Does it mean your wife has to take time off work? How does it affect you or your family?

CLIENT: Well of course it means I can't go to work and it also means that I'm losing money.

This line of questioning has now opened up the consequences behind the abstract statements and offers the therapist the opportunity of following one of two lines of direction:

1 How to get the client out of bed or
2 How to resolve the question of financial hardship.

Both of which, if achieved, will by implication mean a resolution of his depression. This line of questioning does keep your options open and steers away from dead-end conversations. This is very important if the therapist wishes to maintain credibility with the client and family. As with most habituation processes, the client and family soon realise the type and method of questioning used by the therapist and begin to adapt their responses appropriately.

Assessment of current situation (Fig. 3.2b; p. 49) should be an objective collation of all the individual perceptions of the problem and an interactional description of the process which brought about the problem. It is also desirable for the therapist periodically to summarise explicitly what the client and family members are saying as a method of update and objective assessment. This method also verifies any inferences or suppositions made by the therapist or presented by the client. For example:

THERAPIST: Let me see now, am I right in thinking that this is the

---

Consent Form for Video Tape Recording

Name ....

I/We consent to the video tape recording of the interviews of my/our treatment

I/We consent to this recording being shown to professional audiences and any transcripts being used for publication.

I/We understand that prior to use, the recording(s) will as far as possible have all references to personal identity eliminated.

I/We understand that the recording(s) can be erased at my/our request.

Explained to me/us by ....

.... (position held)

Signed .... Date ....

Signed ....

Address ....

....

I consent on behalf of the above named

Signed .... Date ....

Relationship ....

Fig. 4.1   *Consent form for video tape recording*

situation now (followed by a summarisation of what the therapist believes has been presented on 'video camera')?

If the therapist is wrong, the family members will inform her so. If the therapist is right, it is safe to proceed. This method minimises the chances of misinterpretation or serious confusion and uncertainty as treatment proceeds. Ignoring or discarding inadequate, non-specific information can only lead to greater problems in the future for both therapist and family. In cases where global statements are made, for example: 'I'm just not happy', 'I'm not really with it', 'I feel I'm not achieving', it is often best to ask the client to give a recent example of what happened to make him feel that way. The therapist is then always referring back to specific, concrete, observable behaviour which produced the abstract emotions.

It may appear that the empathic response and concretisation are incompatible skills, in that one demands a display of emotional understanding and the other indicates that emotional understanding is not acceptable in interactional terms. Combining these two skills is not based on the fact that they appear to be mutually exclusive but on who is accepting what information. It is perfectly natural and therapeutic for the therapist to respond empathically and express abstracts and emotions, but it is not beneficial for the therapist to accept from the client emotional abstracts on their own as concrete information. The content of the client's abstract or emotional statements can best be utilised to re-enforce the degree of the effect the problem is having on the client and not as a baseline of what is happening to him.

The clinic-based therapist with video equipment *in situ* uses a slightly different method of introduction to the client and family, although all other areas of the initial interview are identical. When the client and family present to the clinic, the previously mentioned standards of courtesy and politeness should still apply. The main difference is that with video equipment there is extra procedural administration in terms of the consent form for videotape recording (Fig. 4.1). It is suggested that the explanation on the consent form and the verbal and signatory consent to the videotape recording being used should be included at the beginning of the tape.

The other major problem encountered is the presence of the video camera. In the author's experience it is difficult to say who is the most aware of the presence of video equipment—the client or the therapist. However, simple measures can be taken to put the family at ease. For example:

THERAPIST: I am sure you are all aware of the video camera but I can tell you, you are not half as aware as I am. The camera is there to record these sessions so that my colleagues and I can record my performance and hopefully improve it. You may be aware of it whirring but that is purely the technicians playing around with the focus and wide-angled lenses. You are probably nervous about the camera but I can assure you, not as nervous as I am. No doubt there are some things you might talk to me about if it wasn't there and I respect that. However, there is no rush to start therapy, so if you want to, I am quite happy to have a general chat until you feel you are ready to start. I would also like to apologise in advance in case the telephone rings. If it does, it just means that one of my colleagues would like me to clarify some particular point about which they are confused.

This statement has pre-warned the family of the practical problems of having a camera in the same room. It also utilises the one-down position, in that the therapist is more anxious than the family. It explains possible interruptions in a normal, honest manner and these are now put in the context of: 'my colleagues are checking up on me', rather than the family thinking: 'Oh my God! What have we said wrong?' The invitation not to disclose certain information on video is again normal. Because the therapist has expressed understanding, the family will now feel more relaxed and therefore be more liable to include that information. The context of 'start when you are ready' also helps relax the family, especially in conjunction with: 'we can have small talk until you are ready' as there will not be any pregnant pauses for which the family might feel guilty. Nor do they feel they are suddenly being thrust into therapy.

Returning to the completion of the assessment form, and the category of management strategy, in a clinic-based situation this is usually done after the front therapist (the one interviewing the family) excuses herself for 10 minutes to consult with colleagues. In the community setting, the management strategy can be assessed in the client's home or the therapist can ask for time to consider all the information she has been given. Management strategy means what you are going to ask the client and family to do in order to achieve the agreed goals. On occasions, using discretion, the therapist may inform the individual and family why they are being asked to attempt certain tasks in order to achieve goals, although generally speaking, the family does not need to know. It is also advisable, as previously stated, to try and ascertain what kind of help the individual and family have sought in order to resolve the situation and also what they themselves have been attempting to do to resolve the problem. The answers to such questions will give the therapist a clear idea of what has been attempted in the past and more importantly, what has been unsuccessful. In order to have an 'odds-on' chance of being successful in therapy, the therapist must avoid the previous attempted solutions simply because they did not work.

By this stage the therapist should have clear information on the presenting problem and the behaviour, interactions and perceptions of each family member in relation to the problem and how previous attempted solutions have failed to make any impact. She should be able to assess in concrete terms what is happening and who is doing it.

In conjunction with the above skills, there are other skills which enhance therapeutic outcome. One is the skill of language. Returning to the earlier analogy of the salesperson and the customer, the salesperson realises that the fact that a particular product is good is not sufficient for a sale to take place. The salesperson knows that it is necessary to associate the product with the needs and desires of the customer. The same product can be sold to different people for different reasons, for example, a car. An analogy frequently used by the Mental Research Institute is that a Rolls-Royce can be sold to both the status-seeker and the customer looking for economy. In both instances the aim is to sell the car, but the sales technique varies greatly. With the status-seeker, the salesperson can appeal to the customer's desire for status and back this with the argument of the price of the car being exclusive, as well as the machinery and finishings. However, he can point out to the economically minded customer that this car is an investment, will last longer than others and maintain its value, thus making it economical. If the values of both customers were to be compared, they are totally irrelevant to each other. However, a good salesperson knows this and can adjust his sales pitch accordingly. Sales pitch is the language the therapist uses. The language of the client is what the client believes in, his values, his commitments and his views on any given situation, that is, his motivation. It is impossible that the client will convey his values, beliefs and attitudes in simplistic terms and the therapist must therefore be consciously aware of how they are expressed in conversation. An example of the differences of language used by clients is as follows. One set of parents state that their rebellious child is causing great concern. On questioning they point out that they feel threatened and anxious when the child openly challenges their authority. Another set of parents may present with their rebellious child stating that they are at their wits' end because they have tried long and hard to identify the emotional need the child is covertly requesting but are unable to identify any particular area they feel they have not fulfilled. Both sets of parents have a rebellious child. In all probability the behavioural patterns of both children are very similar. However, the language in which the parents are presenting the problem varies dramatically. In the first instance the parents are saying they wish to be in control of their child and not have him challenge their parental authority. The other set of parents are saying that the child is disturbed because they have not been able to fulfil some parental emotional duty. Perhaps, as the therapist, you can identify that both sets of parents are using the same attempted solutions, that is, encouragement, discussion, threats or attempting logical reasoning with the child. However, that is the therapist's language and not the language of the client. (Interventions will be discussed in Chapter 7.) When defining the problem with the family, certain key values and attitudes will become apparent, for example, whether or not sacrifice, kindness, martyrdom or other values are involved. It is essential that the therapist picks these up and responds within the same framework. It is useless to tell the economy-minded customer that the car he is about to buy is of great prestige value. If anything, that kind of statement will probably deter him from buying.

Another very useful skill which can be employed throughout the initial and subsequent sessions is that of neutrality. Neutrality is what it says, being neutral. Since the therapist is confronted with two or more differing perceptions of the same problem, it is easy to believe more strongly in one perception than another. However, if this happens, the therapist's language will soon indicate this and the client and family will be able to pick this up. For example:

WIFE: He beats me up.
THERAPIST: That's not very nice.
THERAPIST TO HUSBAND: Why do you beat her up?
HUSBAND: Well, she really gets on my nerves.
THERAPIST: You do of course realise assault is a criminal offence?

In this case neutrality has been breached immediately. By

indicating that such interactions are illegal, even when instigated by the husband, the therapist has aligned herself to the wife's cause, irrespective of the interactions preceding the physical violence. As a result, in all probability the husband will feel alienated from therapy and perhaps even a scapegoat. If this occurs then the therapist can no longer count on the husband's co-operation in trying to overcome the problem as the husband's perception of the therapist, depending on the sex of the therapist, is either: 'Women stick together' or: 'He didn't understand. He should have realised what it's like.' A simple way of testing the therapist's neutrality is unfortunately by hindsight. If at the end of a session, the therapist came out and an independent observer went in and said to each individual: 'Whose side do you think the therapist was on, if any?' then all the participants should be able to respond: 'I thought she was on my side.' Although total neutrality is very difficult to achieve, it should be borne in mind so that the therapist does not consciously side or appear to side with one participant or the other.

Validation is another skill which should be used throughout all sessions. It means acknowledging and accepting the perceptions and statements made by each and every participant and is a combination of neutrality and empathy. Each individual must feel a useful and important contributor to therapy and this can best be achieved by acknowledging each statement as it arises. As an example, in a situation where there is marital disharmony and arguments:

THERAPIST TO DAUGHTER: From what your parents say they seem to be arguing a lot. How does this affect you?
DAUGHTER: Well, it really upsets me. I don't like seeing it and I feel as if I'm being left out—as if I didn't exist.
THERAPIST: That's a very interesting and important point. Thank you very much. Perhaps we should look at what your parents think about this situation.
THERAPIST TO PARENTS: Were you aware that your daughter could hear the arguments?

If the parents indicate that they were aware that their daughter could overhear their arguments, then this gives the therapist an indication of the attitudes and beliefs of the parents. If the parents indicate that they were not aware their daughter could overhear their arguments, then that gives an added leverage in using the daughter in therapeutic terms to mediate or conciliate. Alternatively it may bring into play an outside factor which the parents had not considered and therefore may be utilised in some form to decrease or stop the arguments. Another form of validation, which is slightly more difficult to handle, could be as follows. In this instance the marital disharmony is based on the father's drinking and aggression and the mother's inability to handle this:

THERAPIST TO MOTHER: How do you see the problem affecting you?

MOTHER: It's the same every Saturday night. When he comes home around 11 o'clock from work, it's obvious he's spent the last four hours down the pub and then he demands his dinner.

THERAPIST TO MOTHER: That must be pretty tough for you. I imagine that, like most wives, you have your routine to follow to get through the amount of work most women seem to have to do.

THERAPIST TO FATHER: How do you see the problem?

FATHER: Well, it's no wonder I spend half my time down the pub. If I come home, it's nothing but nag, nag, nag. It's enough to drive a man to drink. I get enough hassle at work without having to put up with it at home.

THERAPIST TO FATHER: Well, I can certainly see the kind of pressures you're under and I must admit I certainly wouldn't like to be under all these pressures. It's nice to have time to relax and unwind at the end of a hard day.

The therapist has validated both viewpoints, however extreme, and has also indicated a basic understanding of the causations surrounding their individual perceptions. In order to finalise the statements offered by this couple, the therapist must somehow attempt to bring both perceptions into one statement which could apply to both. Thus the therapist identifies common ground and imparts some understanding to each partner of the other's problem. For example, in the above case:

THERAPIST TO MOTHER AND FATHER: I really do understand the problems both of you are having and the difficulty you are both experiencing. It seems that both of you are under quite extreme pressures in your daily routines and you both feel you need to wind down from these pressures before you can devote time to enjoying each other's company.

This statement is deliberately middle-of-the-road so that it applies to each partner and each can identify it as a fair summary of how they feel and perceive the problems.

These skills of concretisation, problem identification, neutrality, language and validity all help the therapist to retain a relatively objective viewpoint rather than become enmeshed in the problem area of emotions and feelings. It can be extremely hard to avoid situations where clients ask for the therapist's opinion on their feelings, implied in such a way as to make it quite clear that if the therapist does not agree with their evaluation of their emotions, they will think: 'You don't understand.' An example of this is when the therapist is asked by one of the parties involved in escalating arguments: 'Do you think I'm right in feeling as angry as I do?' Whichever way the therapist answers this question can easily be seen by either party as a breach of neutrality and the aggrieved party could well subsequently co-operate less with the therapist. The easiest method of maintaining neutrality while at the same time validating this person would be to state: 'Yes, I am sure that you do feel immense degrees of anger.' If the client pursues the matter, that is: 'Very well, but do *you* think I'm right to feel angry?', then in order for the therapist to maintain integrity and credibility to both partners, a common therapeutic response would be: 'I honestly couldn't say whether you are right or wrong, just as I cannot say your spouse is right or wrong. It is impossible for me to judge as I am not present before and during such arguments. However, I certainly do accept that this is the way you feel and it seems to me that you are both experiencing intense emotions which seem to make reconciliation during an argument harder to achieve. I think it would be much more beneficial to both of you if we were to concentrate at this moment, not on the intensity of the emotions you obviously experience, but rather on methods of attempting to avoid these situations in the first place.' By employing a one-down position and re-enforcing validity, the therapist is stating that she is unable to answer that particular question due to her absence at the time of the incident. This should block continued pursuance of that particular question. Depending on the degree of frustration or anger expressed by the questioner, then the therapist may or may not pursue this by using even more validation. The therapist could of course use the skill of concretisation in this instance and, when faced with the original question, ask: 'How does this degree of anger actually affect you? Is there anything you feel compelled to do or say at that time?' Or: 'What happens when you get extremely angry? What do you do? What does your spouse do?' Thus the client is channelled into giving the therapist more information without feeling that she does not understand or empathise.

Another useful method of dealing with abstract questions, especially those of a diagnostic nature, is to respond in one of three ways in relation to the three categories of problems described in Chapter 3. These are: 'Is there anything you would like to start doing which (the problem) stops you doing?', 'Is there anything you would like to stop doing which (the problem) makes it impossible for you to do?', or 'Is there anything you are doing now which you would like to do differently but because of (the problem) you are unable to?' These are the main problems that may be encountered during an initial interview and the skills that are necessary in order to minimise these problems. There are of course many other skills and techniques in family therapy which can be utilised during the initial interview but in terms of getting clear, precise and therapeutically useful information these are the main ones.

The initial interview can take anywhere between half an hour and one and a half hours. This obviously depends on the clarity and specificity of the information given. In cases when a client is well aware of the problem, of the behaviours surrounding the problem and is in a position to give clear information as requested, the initial interview time can be minimal. However, at the other extreme, when a client is aware of the presenting problem but not of the interactions, then it will obviously take longer to establish details, especially in family cases if there are varying and often extreme viewpoints on one particular problem. As in surgery, if the surgeon states: 'Your operation should take approximately half an hour', and he completes the operation in a quarter of an hour, he is certainly not expected to wait around for a quarter of an hour until his estimated time is up. Nor is he expected to stop the operation and sew up after half an hour if he encounters problems which require more time in surgery. Likewise with therapy, rigid adherence to any time limit is inappropriate. In some cases the client may continue to express a need to talk to the therapist and if further new information is forthcoming, then by all means proceed. However, should no new information be forthcoming, then it is more appropriate to wind up that particular session there and then. This can best be done by using one of several statements, such as: 'It seems to me that we have gone as far as we can today so I think we should leave it at that.' Or: 'I think I've got enough information to keep me going so if you like I will go away and digest this.' In terms of courtesy and again to re-enforce validation, it is useful to leave with a comment such as: 'Thank you very much for all the useful information you have given me and I am sure this will help me gain a clearer picture.'

Some therapists prefer to see the initial interview as being purely information-gathering, followed by a period of time in which the information is sifted and analysed. They then proceed to the second session. However, other, mainly clinic-based therapists, due to their practical setting, prefer to institute tasks at the end of the first session. If at the end of the first session the therapist feels able to formulate and institute tasks, then there is no reason why she should not do so.

However, before the therapist can do this, she needs to know the goals of therapy. It is not in keeping with the process of therapy if the therapist or client sets goals without discussing them with each other. Therefore goal-setting is a skill. It does not necessarily follow that once a clear definition of the problem and specific attempted solutions have been identified, goals are a natural progression. In many cases a couple will disagree on the definition of the problem or may even agree on the definition but have differing goals. For example, the previously mentioned couple caught up in the circularity of his drinking and her nagging have different definitions of the problem. They also have different solutions and as a result, different goals. In this example, the husband would see the solution as his wife no longer nagging him, whereas the wife would see the solution as the husband's stopping drinking. The therapist must take into account each of the solutions proposed in order to formulate a goal of her own. With some couples it is possible to amalgamate both solutions into a goal. For example, would the husband be prepared to stop or cut down drinking if the wife stopped or cut down nagging? Because of the nature of arguments it is unusual for both to agree to this, therefore it may be best to propose both solutions in sequence. The husband stops drinking for one week, then the wife stops nagging for one week in order to see which affords the greatest difference to both. Quite often a good goal is the gradual diminishment of the problem. However the therapist should always be wary of allowing unrealistic goals to be set. For example:

THERAPIST: What do you think we should aim at as our goal?
CLIENT: I want to feel better—to be able never to have depression again. (Unrealistic)
THERAPIST: Well, that may be aiming a bit high. What would be realistic in terms of the present situation?

The therapist must consider what is normal and adjust the goal accordingly. In the above instance, 30 years of excellent therapy would still not guarantee the goal. Goals should be achievable relatively rapidly and then if necessary further goals could be set. If the client is unable to set concrete, realistic goals then the therapist can enquire what would be a movement in the right direction, again keeping to concrete interactional language. The goal should be logical in relation to the overall problem, pleasing to the client in that progress can be identified on achievement and desirable for attaining resolution of the problem.

It is also advisable at the end of the initial session for the client to be informed of the proposed interval between sessions, that is one week, two weeks, three weeks etc. It is entirely at the therapist's discretion which is chosen. Less than one week and over four weeks tend to be non-therapeutic, firstly, because it takes at least a week to implement behavioural change, for the client to be aware of this, taste the rewards and want more. More than four weeks and the client may slip back into old habits due to non-re-enforcement or lack of new goals. Much depends on the administrative and clinical commitments of the therapist.

Each session should be recorded in writing and the initial assessment sent to the referring agency, GP, psychiatrist or other professionals involved. For clinic-based therapists with video equipment, time allocated for playback is essential. If the therapist has no co-therapy team during the session, then evaluation can take place on replay. For community-based therapists this video facility in all probability does not exist. It is useful to have clinical team meetings where difficult cases can be discussed with colleagues providing the co-therapy evaluation. Unfortunately, this again impinges on clinical time. A common and relatively successful compromise is that when difficulty is being experienced by the community-based therapist, she can have the option of taking a co-therapist with her on the next session to evaluate *in situ.*

Summary

This chapter has looked at the need to be prepared by having as much clear, precise and specific information as possible. The desirability of having objective, unbiased perception was stressed. Such skills as neutrality, problem identification, validity, concretisation and language help to elicit factual, observable information rather than the more abstract type. Examples were given of each of these skills. It should be noted that although these skills may seem separate and disjointed, they overlap and can be used in conjunction with one another. Practice in this area makes for smoother therapy.

The need for realistic, achievable goals is paramount in order to motivate the client towards trying.

The importance of the initial interview is that it sets the pace, direction and atmosphere for future sessions, thus removing the need for re-establishing them on each visit.

An over-riding skill is professional courtesy and discretion, which will help establish a more therapeutic relationship, thus making the therapist's job easier.

Exercises

1 Do you ask all family members present for their viewpoint on the problem?
2 Do you identify what the problem is rather than the diagnosis?
3 In your next clinical session, attempt to avoid descriptive, abstract terms. It is difficult.
4 Question the client when he talks of 'depression' and such abstracts. For example: 'How does this affect you?'
5 At the end of each session, try to evaluate how neutral you were.

6 After implementing the above, has the problem area become any clearer to you or the family?

7 Are the client's and family's goals of treatment the same as yours? If not, discuss this with the family.

These exercises help to clarify any misunderstanding that may evolve due to assumption or implication on either side. Self-assessment, like therapy, is on-going and the need to evaluate your own performance is never-ending. As the above skills are practised then, like riding a bike, it gets easier until you do not have to think about it.

Reference

MacPhail, W. D. (1986). Skills in family therapy, *Nursing Times*; 82:26:49.

5

Where Now?

If you wish to head west as fast as possible, your first step should be in a westerly direction. Likewise in therapy; the direction and speed the therapist now travels are greatly influenced by the skills, techniques and options used during the first visit.

Part of the assessment used by health visitors requires them: 'to analyse, interpret, compare and synthesise this range of information in order to compile an assessment ...' (Orr, 1985). Analysing and interpreting the information is a heavy burden at the best of times, which relies on the assessor's ability to do this, presumably based on previous experience—not very comforting for the newly appointed assessor. It also opens wide the possibility of mis-analysis and misinterpretation. Health visitors are also requested to carry out 'core assessments for each individual' (Orr, 1985) where there are different or conflicting needs within the family. As can be seen from the examples of conflicting needs given in Chapter 4, a common theme can readily be identified using the skills of neutrality and validity. Another feature of the above assessment programme is that: 'the health visitor does not carry out ideas with the child herself as this can make the parents feel inadequate' (Orr, 1985). In situations where the problem centres around the parent–child relationship, this statement would appear to exclude an obvious avenue of possible therapy. Each of the above-mentioned statements minimises effective therapy and to a large degree will actually increase the length of time the assessor spends obtaining precise information. The need for analysis and interpretation may also lead to personal biases interfering with goals. It is simpler and more effective to avoid these traps by minimising analysis. Many other areas of the health visitors' assessment programme are identical to those of the psychiatric therapist, for example, the need to identify cultural variables and the acceptance of the client's perceptions.

In district nursing it is recommended that the treatment plan should 'be integrated into the main plan ... unless the mental disturbance is such that it overshadows all other aspects of the patient's illness' (Baly, 1981). Although it is indicated that this treatment will probably be carried out by other professionals such as 'social workers or the community psychiatric nurse' (Baly, 1981), district nurses are advised to identify the primary cause of the psychiatric illness.

In terms of therapeutic outcome, much of the time spent by other professionals, for example health visitors and district nurses, can create a bias in referral to psychiatry, albeit an unconscious one, which, if acted on by the psychiatric therapist at face value, will become a time-consuming exercise which will probably not prove beneficial in the end. Therefore the important question is not who is giving the information but rather what is the calibre of the information? Although the above two examples from health visiting and district nursing involve recognising and evaluating the impact of illness on the family, the methods used also indicate which avenues remain open and/or shut.

Apart from the professional's perception of the illness or problem, the client has probably also been assessing the assessor and may now have some idea of the direction of therapy and whether or not he believes he is likely to suceed. The author does not know of any research done in this area. Perhaps it would be constructive and interesting to see how accurately clients can predict outcome of therapy before and following the first interview.

As mentioned earlier (p.69), some therapists prefer to include task-setting at the end of the initial interview, whereas others prefer to have the opportunity to discuss this matter with colleagues. Clinic-based therapists usually have the advantage of a team behind a two-way mirror or watching closed circuit television and probably find it easier to formulate tasks as the first session progresses. Community-based therapists working in pairs can use strategies at the end of the first session to discuss possible tasks. They can request 10 minutes to discuss the matter themselves or while the client makes a cup of tea. However the situation for the sole therapist in the community is very different. There can either be rigid adherence to the principle of not setting tasks until deliberation with colleagues has taken place or, if the therapist feels sufficiently confident, she can take a flexible approach to task-setting where appropriate.

The function of task-setting is directly or indirectly to achieve the goal or goals previously set. The therapist must pay attention to the language used by the client to be successful. As in the example of the two men wishing to buy a Rolls-Royce (p. 63), it is totally inappropriate for the salesperson to advise the status seeker that the best advantage of the car is economy. Therefore the identified task must be based in terms of the client's perception of the problem. It is also important to remember information about the client's previous attempted solutions which will indicate avenues and methods which have not succeeded. It is pointless for the therapist to re-enforce methods the client already knows do not work. If re-enforcement takes place the client will probably begin to lose faith in the therapist and withdraw his co-operation. For example, if a car is going in the wrong direction, the solution would be to reverse the car although respite could be gained by stopping the car from going any further. The therapist should be able to gain a clear picture of the direction the client is pursuing from his perception of his illness or problem and his attempted solutions. To be effective the therapist should then indicate a change in direction. That is, a reverse direction which is logical and sensible in the client's language or failing this, at least a temporary halt in the direction currently being pursued. It will obviously be very difficult to convince the client that his attempted solutions have not taken him in the right direction as this will probably go against his perception of the problem. The premise is that if the client knew he was attempting the wrong solution, he would not be attempting it. The task must also centre around the specific interactional aspects of the problem or symptoms. In the case of a man suffering from depression following redundancy five years ago, it would be therapeutically ineffectual to centre tasks around his redundancy alone. It would be more therapeutic to evolve tasks relating to the current depression, with a view to resolving the present psychological problems which he has had since redundancy.

An example of how things can consistently go wrong by taking the first step in the wrong direction is the following extract from a case history. This case will be used for further examples in later chapters to show the development of the family in response to appropriate family therapy techniques and skills.

Mrs Mary Walker was 21 with two sons, Jonathan, aged 3 years and David, aged 17 months. Mary was referred to the community psychiatric nurse following her attendance at a casualty department stating she could not cope with the children. She was sent home to await psychiatric assessment the following day and Jonathan was kept in hospital to give Mary short-term relief. The family was living in a small two-bedroomed council flat. She had a part-time job in the evenings. Her husband George, aged 23 years, worked full-time in manual employment.

At the initial assessment the community psychiatric nurse stated that Mrs Walker had puerperal depression, was immature and as a result could not cope with Jonathan. It was noted that since David was born Jonathan had become more overtly aggressive both to his mother and to his brother. The management plan at that time was to offer support to the family. Mary was visited by the community psychiatric nurse on a daily basis for 1 week initially. The nurse reported that at first things began to improve but then deteriorated to the point where George was unable to go to work as Mary had become non-coping and had developed a non-eating disorder.

Within 1 month of the initial referral Jonathan had been referred to a day nursery 2 days a week. Within a fortnight of this Mary indicated to the community psychiatric nurse that she was deliberately attempting to harm Jonathan.

Within 2 months of the initial referral Mary had been referred to a psychoanalyst/clinical assistant who ran special groups for mothers experiencing problems with new babies. Jonathan's attendance at the day nursery increased to full-time. At this time, Mary was transferred to another community psychiatric nurse as the first nurse left the service. Mary was reported as stating: 'I feel like a parcel being handed round for help.' A month after the second community psychiatric nurse became involved, the Walkers were referred to the local housing officer with a view to re-housing to larger accommodation, on the premise that accommodation was a major factor in the problem. Two weeks later it was reported that the general family situation was deteriorating with Mary reporting that violence toward Jonathan by her was on the increase. At this time a third community psychiatric nurse was introduced as the second nurse left the service.

Within 5 months of the initial referral, a myriad of professionals was involved: GP, psychoanalyst, psychiatrist, community psychiatric nurse, health visitor, divisional social worker and two social workers attached to the nursery Jonathan attended. Mrs Walker was now reported to be attempting suicide by taking overdoses.

Six months following initial referral there was a case conference attended by all professionals involved at which it was decided to minimise the amount of professionals visiting, as opposed to professionals involved, as some professionals were visiting unauthorised. Those authorised to visit were the GP and the community psychiatric nurse. It was also noted that there appeared to be a sexual problem between Mr and Mrs Walker.

Seven months after the initial referral, the Walkers were re-housed but the situation did not improve, thus excluding housing as a major cause of the problem.

Eight months after the initial referral, the community psychiatric nurse decided that the situation was one of a typical see-saw marriage, that is, complementary coping and non-coping by each partner in turn.

One year after the initial referral, due to non-progress or even deterioration, a multidisciplinary crisis intervention visit took place. The crisis intervention team recommended that a contract should be drawn up and the family should undertake four sessions of therapy.

This is an excellent example of incomplete and inconclusive information leading to the professionals being inconclusive in their own treatment programme. As Mary herself stated: 'I am confused by all the different advice I get.' Hence the decision to cut down the number of professionals involved. The crisis intervention team's recommendations were seen by Mary as even more differing advice.

The unfortunate aspect of this case is that each professional who visited the family sought information which re-enforced his or her own perception of the problem. Nobody had actually seen the family as a family. There were various clues which indicated that despite Mary's attempted solutions, things were not getting better but worse. She had been continually informed by the professionals that she must 'try to get better' or her 'children would be removed into care'. It would be fair to say that although doing their best, the professionals involved did not recognise Mary's perception of the problem, the impact it was having on the family and they did not use such skills as neutrality and validity. As a result, the tasks set, although logical and sensible to the professionals, were obviously not in the client's language but purely a re-enforcement of an attempted solution which did not work.

At the first of the sessions instituted by the crisis intervention team it was decided that the current community psychiatric nurse should act as front therapist. A genogram (Fig. 5.1) was used in order to try and simplify the amount of information the Walker

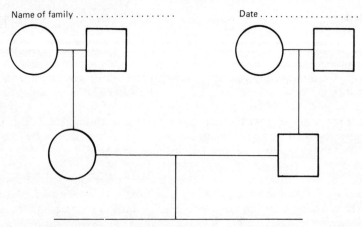

Fig. 5.1   *Three-generational genogram*

family was providing. A genogram is a map, usually three-gener-ational, of the people composing the nuclear and extended family unit. There is room for additional information which the family or therapist considers important in terms of functioning. As can be seen from the Walkers' genogram (Fig. 5.2), George identified that he was the victim of child abuse and Mary indicated that she was the victim of child sexual abuse by her stepfather. Both Mary and George had mothers who were still alive, although Mary's mother had no contact with the family. It is interesting that Mary pushed her stepfather downstairs, which apparently led to a coronary from which he later died. Other interesting information is that Mary did not or was not allowed to hold Jonathan when he was born as he was taken to a separate room without any explanation. It also transpired that George and his mother decided on the name of the baby and presented Mary with a *fait accompli*.

As can be seen from this limited information, a wealth of possibilities commonly called hypotheses, could be developed, depending on the perception or model of the professional. Un-fortunately, each professional did hypothesise and came up with (what seemed to each of them) very logical and obvious hypo-theses. The psychoanalyst felt that the current situation was a result of childhood traumas of both Mary and George. The GP did not really know what to do as intensive support did not work. The social workers were involved in Jonathan's day care, re-

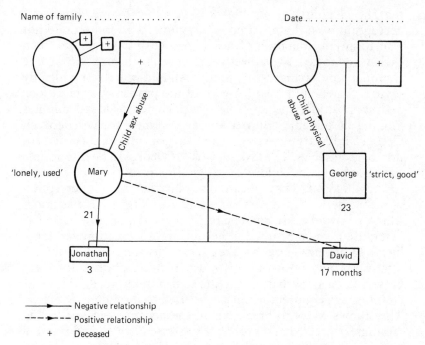

Name of family . . . .   Date . . . .

'lonely, used'   Mary   George   'strict, good'

Child sex abuse

Child physical abuse

21

23

Jonathan   David

3   17 months

———▶— Negative relationship

- - -▶- - - Positive relationship

+   Deceased

Fig. 5.2   *The Walker family genogram*

housing and the possibility of taking Jonathan into care. The health visitor was concerned regarding possible abuse of Jonathan and the effect the family situation would have on the children's development. The community psychiatric nurse was concerned regarding the varying symptoms mentioned by Mary. However, nobody had looked at the current situation, interactions and possible solutions, which although they seemed to be logical, were in fact promoting the current situation. Mary was clearly anxious due to her inability to cope and the resultant depression. George was 'fed up with it all' and the children were also exhibiting signs that they were not happy with the current situation.

The aim of the first therapy session was to clarify the information received in such a way as to be specific at the same time as validating and remaining neutral. At the end of the first session it was identified that George's perception of the problem was that Mary was a baby batterer. Mary's perception of the problem was that she felt guilty as a result of not being able to cope. Jonathan's perception was: 'I am scared of Mummy'. This in itself did not lead to any formulation of tasks. George and Mary were then each asked to give two adjectives to describe themselves. George responded by saying: 'strict and good' and Mary responded by saying: 'lonely and used'. Aware of the pitfalls of implications and supposition, the therapists decided to spend 10 minutes looking at possible connections or common themes between George and Mary's perception of the problem and their perception of themselves. The task set was for George to be responsible for disciplining the children. George already saw himself as being strict, which could have meant disciplinarian, but his perception was that he was in control and therefore discipline was good. Mary, who had a history of being sexually abused, saw herself as being used which resulted in her feelings of isolation and loneliness. By asking George to take over the discipline role within the family, his perception of Mary must change as she can no longer be seen as a baby batterer if she had nothing to do with disciplining the children, neither is he used to discipline by proxy. This allows Mary to break out of the negative cycle of feeling anxious, depressed and probably frustrated, which had resulted in violence towards Jonathan.

The effect of the task was to change the perception George and Mary had of each other as well as of themselves. In George's language, despite being the victim of child abuse himself, now he has matured and has children of his own, he will not over-discipline them because he knows how much discipline he would have liked as a child. This is both logical and realistic for George as he states he is already 'fed up' with Mary's over-disciplining. From Mary's point of view, there is an empathic response; she has a lot on her plate as a wife and mother and is obviously unable to control her physical involvement with Jonathan, so the best thing she could do would be to stay away from him. She would then no longer feel used by George in disciplining the children, which she had indicated earlier by stating: 'He's never around to discipline them. He doesn't understand.' So that Mary would no longer perceive herself as being lonely, we added that although George was responsible for discipline, they should both get together in the evenings and discuss the children's behaviour as it affected Mary. In this way the task complied with their individual perceptions of the problem and both parents remained involved with the children and also had the feeling that they were working together. Other qualitative statements were made by the therapist such as: 'Try this for the time being and see if it works.' This is a realistic statement, although the time limit is abstract, and is also partially a re-enforcement of the one-down position in that the therapist is not always right. Before the delivery of this task, the water was tested in terms of the client's responses in the following manner:

THERAPIST: Correct me if I'm wrong, George, but it seems to me that you place some importance on bringing up children right. It seems that you value discipline as a parent. This seems quite right to me because can you imagine what kind of world we would live in if children didn't have discipline?

GEORGE: Yes, discipline is important. I used to get leathered when I was a child but it didn't do me any harm.

THERAPIST: Mary, it seems to me that, like most mothers, being close to your children sometimes gets to be a bit overpowering to the point where you just get frustrated with them. I think most mothers would like at one point or another to strangle their children, but they don't—just like you. What do you think would happen if you stopped disciplining the children?

MARY: Well, of course I don't like doing it—it gets out of control, but if I don't they will just run wild.

THERAPIST: How would you feel if George were to do it for you?

MARY: That would suit me fine.

Both agree that discipline is important. From each individual's perception, George would be quite happy doing it whereas Mary feels very much under pressure whilst issuing discipline. The task has therefore been formulated by on-going discussion and the delivery made. The family were then asked to try this method for 2 weeks with the proviso that if things went wrong in that area or any other, they should phone the therapist for guidance. Again this is realistic as the therapist is asking the clients to go away and change their behaviours, which may or may not work. It is therefore appropriate for them to have access if they believe things are going wrong. Although this task was both logical and appropriate to the individuals' perceptions, it does not necess-arily mean that the family will come back with a successful outcome. The change of behaviour within the nuclear family will have an influence on both the extended and social families. In the Walkers' case they did return with some improvement although they later related to the therapist that some members of the extended family advised against following the professional advice. It also transpired from a later interview that other professionals had maintained telephone contact and, unaware of the purpose of the task-setting, actively though unconsciously had undermined the family's therapeutic relationship with the therapist. This was mainly because the health visitor and social workers did not understand the reasons behind the therapist's evident although transient intention of separating mother and child in terms of disciplining. From their professional perception it would be detrimental to separate mother and child and their own anxieties probably caused a negating effect in their conversations with the client. It also transpired that George's mother had a very strong influence within the family and this was not accounted for initially. She did her best to undermine any form of task-setting by the therapist.

All of this was understandable in terms of psychosocial transition. The equilibrium or status quo of the family for the previous year had been that George had been sacrificial in terms of trying to run the family, which was his wife's responsibility, and hold down a job at the same time. This gave the appearance that George was being very protective and providing towards his family, which fitted in with the perception of George's side of the nuclear family and family of origin. Because Mary had had a bad relationship with her mother-in-law since the birth of Jonathan it also served to denigrate Mary's coping abilities in the eyes of George's side of the family. Any change in behaviour could be seen by those professionals who remained in contact as possibly heading towards disaster. It became apparent later in therapy that comments had been made by other professionals, such as: 'You shouldn't listen to them. They don't know what they are talking about' or: 'They don't understand what you've got to put up with.'

It therefore becomes apparent that the therapist should consider the avenues of communication open to the client at the time of task-setting. For example, George and Mary had continued access to George's mother and the GP, which the therapist knew about. However they also had access to agencies which had been previously involved, as well as their social family. It is therefore advisable when asking who is involved to make a clear differentiation between those actively or passively involved and those involved physically or from a distance. Had the therapist been aware of the telephone conversations between Mary and the other agencies she could have made the task-setting more effective by stating: 'I am sure that other agencies or professionals will possibly disagree with this but this is probably because they don't understand why I am asking you to do this and on the surface it appears to go against their beliefs.' This form of prediction minimises the effect of 'good intentions' and at the same time predicts their outcome. It also shows the client that you have taken all other viewpoints into consideration and this can only deepen the therapeutic relationship between therapist and client.

This simplistic approach of task-setting can be used with some clients as long as it is appropriate in terms of the client's language. For example:

CLIENT: I want to stop smoking.

THERAPIST: What makes you want to stop smoking?

CLIENT: Nowadays it's antisocial and anyway I want to save money; I'm getting married.

THERAPIST: Why don't you just not buy any cigarettes and put the money in a jar instead?

CLIENT: I never thought of that. I'll give it a try.

THERAPIST: It's probably too obvious and you've probably tried it before. If it doesn't work, that's OK. Come back and we'll talk about other methods.

In this case the client did not come back and one year later he still had not re-started smoking.

One of the major obstacles encountered by therapists is that of the client's motivation towards change. It is almost certainly the experience of every therapist that at least one case has failed dismally and you have said: 'The client wasn't motivated.' It is the author's belief that all clients have motivation and if there is a successful outcome to therapy then the motivation has been reached. However, if the result of therapy is failure, then the motivation has not been reached. It is the therapist's responsibility to motivate the client and if this does not happen, then the therapist should look to herself rather than to the client. It is all too easy to recall situations where failure of therapy has been justified by statements of: 'Well, of course he is a chronic...' or 'He is a difficult client.' These statements evoke the response of anecdotal definitions, that is, that chronicity is purely the pessimistic view of the therapist in light of the failure of other treatments and difficulty is when the therapist does not understand. On a more simple level, one does not catch chronic schizophrenia or chronic depression. The word 'chronic' is adjectival or descriptive and serves to give a guideline of how long attempted solutions have been tried. In other words, all previous therapies from whichever model have failed to identify and/or use the correct solutions. In subjective terms, if this concept is followed through then the person who states that the client is chronic is, from her perception, stating that there is no cure. This implies that once illness has struck, in chronic terms, there is no possibility of improvement of quality of life. If the professionals who use such words as 'chronic' or 'difficult' were confronted with the implications of their verbal definitions, I would imagine that a large majority would disagree with the above definition and state that they hope by their intervention or involvement to raise the level of functioning.

In general terms, to enhance motivation the therapist should primarily use the client's language, empathy, the one-down position, neutrality and validation. These skills on their own will promote an atmosphere between client and therapist of understanding; understanding will promote the deepening of the relationship. One of the biggest drawbacks to community workers, especially nurses, in the use of empathy and creating deeper relationships is that they believe, albeit implicitly, that clients are manipulative and psychopathic. The author can see no other justification for the reticence and sometimes abhorrence of community workers in refusing to give away personal details in the treatment of others. The therapist can only lose control when she gives control away. Another level of motivation may be in situations where the therapist has inadvertently empathised to the point where the client perceives the therapist as a friend rather than somebody instituting change and to a large degree does not follow the tasks. In this situation a way of motivating the client toward achieving goals and tasks is to adopt the 'go slow' theory. This involves a superficial re-assessment of the situation by the therapist. In terms of achievement the therapist can assume the responsibility for lack of success (incorporating one-down) and actually propose that she has been asking for too great a change in too short a time. The logical outcome is therefore that the therapist goes slow. For example:

THERAPIST: It seems to me that despite coming weekly for the last 2 months no real progress has been achieved. This is very unfortunate because I think that I've probably been asking too much of you. In fact I know I must be asking too much of you because if I were asking what you are able to do, I know you would have done it. Therefore I think in future we should go slow. By going slow I mean that we cut down on the times I visit and we reduce the levels of the tasks I set you. I'm sorry I have been asking too much too soon but how about if I meet you in 3 weeks' instead of 1 week?

When the relationship between therapist and client has evolved in such a way that it interferes with therapy, this is one of the major motivation enhancers. From the client's point of view he must provide some form of improvement, otherwise, as seen above, he is implying that the therapist is asking too much. This skill can also be used earlier on in therapy if the client becomes unrealistic in his own goals, aims of therapy or task-setting. This technique, to a large extent, also deals with the secondary gains of illness, as explained in psychosocial transition (p. 12). It can also imply indefinite treatment. For example:

THERAPIST: How much weight have you lost/gained in the last week?
CLIENT: Well I've been trying really hard but I've been unable to lose/gain any.

As the therapist is taking full responsibility for the lack of progress, the client is now faced with a new dilemma: to lose the input that he values or to offer some form of progress to maintain the therapist in therapy. In terms of the deepening relationship, the client must provide some form of identifiable concrete improvement if he wishes the relationship to continue. In the short-term the therapist actually excuses the client from making progress, again by taking the responsibility herself. Either way the client is free to adopt a more positive attitude toward progress.

Even if this tactic fails, the therapist can still go back to the one-down position and state: 'I am very sorry. I must have misperceived the situation. I felt we were getting nowhere. Could you tell me how you feel we are progressing?'

Motivation is also commonly linked in the minds of professionals with resistance. The best advice for dealing with resistance is to avoid it in the first place. This can be done by a variety of methods whenever the therapist feels a controversial subject may arise or when she believes the client is non-accepting of her viewpoint. This can best be avoided by summarising. Summarising can and should be done with no specific restriction on how often but the author recommends it should be done at the approximate end of any given topic. For example:

THERAPIST: Can I just get clear in my head what I think you have discussed so far?'

or: Correct me if I'm wrong but I believe that...

or: Correct me if I'm wrong but are you saying that...?

This ensures that the information you have received and are interpreting is fed back to the client within his perception. If you have misinterpreted it means that you have only done so for the last 5, 10 or 15 minutes. It is therefore much easier to go back and say: 'I'm sorry. I totally misunderstood that. Could you summarise it yourself?'

One of the main problems in assessment and consecutive treatment sessions is that the therapist will make assumptions and read meanings into words or statements which may or may not be there. It is essential in terms of semantics that the therapist should clarify any statement which could lead to any form of misunderstanding. For example, a man states that he no longer loves his wife. The therapist believes that because the man no longer loves his wife in general terms this means that there is no emotional attachment, nor as a result is there any physical i.e. sexual attachment. In such a case the therapist is assuming that love means an emotional attachment upon which the entire physical, sexual, and emotional relationship is based. However, from the client's point of view, it may only mean that there is no sexual attachment due to a variety of other problems. The author can recall an incident when a female client gave a 2-hour tirade about her husband's lack of emotion, lack of sexual contact, lack of physical contact, lack of understanding and how this had been going on for the last 7 years. The therapist advised the client to consider whether or not she wished the relationship to continue and the client replied: 'But of course, I love him.' Because of her objections about virtually all aspects of the relationship, the therapist assumed that there was therefore no love between the couple—physical, sexual or emotional—in which case a distinct possibility would have been the dissolution of the relationship. However the client asserted that there was a very high degree of love. Therefore assumptions and implications should be made explicit rather than left open to misinterpretation.

The author believes that the therapist should only provide guidelines and parameters for therapy. The client should take responsibility for the direction and speed at which the solution is found within these parameters. The problem is the client's and the solution must be the client's also. The therapist is only there to facilitate the client reaching the solution. A fair guide to successful therapy is judged on who is working the hardest. If it is the therapist, then she is taking too much responsibility for seeking the solution. To use an American epigram, if the therapist is sweating, then the therapy is wrong. The therapist should guide the client towards a method of perception which enables him to reach the solution. If the therapist achieves the solution and the client is aware of this, he then has the option of relapse. It is not a learning experience for the client and if the therapist's solution does not work, it is not the client's fault. This could destroy any positive relationship of trust that has been engendered between therapist and client.

Another baseline for therapy could be the quotation: 'Conserve your powers. Be like the expansive ocean, which quietly absorbs the rivers of the senses' (Hua, 1974).

Having gained the initial information the direction to follow can be planned in advance based on that information. It is essential in all interviews and sessions for the therapist to have clear goals which she intends to achieve by the end of the session. If not, therapy will become like a meandering river following the contours of the country without ever getting anywhere. The second and subsequent sessions should be planned in advance with clear objectives in mind and a precise idea of which specific issues to follow as well as which issues from the first session require clarification. This can best be introduced by stating: 'I have had time to think about what you said last time and with the benefit of hindsight I find that I am still a bit muddled about (whatever issue).' In terms of therapy it is suicidal to play it by ear. Playing it by ear, in contrast to deliberate case-planning, means that the therapist does not really have any idea of or, more importantly, control over the direction in which therapy is going. It is only fair that if the client is set tasks and goals to achieve within a limited number of sessions, the therapist also accepts that she has a limited amount of time to achieve her goals and objectives or help the client achieve his.

These then are the general guidelines that dictate the direction to take in terms of therapy and information received from the client and family. However, in terms of the therapist's perform-ance, there are other issues that can and should be explored. On-going self-assessment is an integral part of therapy. If the therapist felt uneasy at any point of the initial interview then, if possible, discussion should take place with colleagues to explore the reason for the unease. It may be that the cause lies within the therapist's own personal experience or it may have been an inappropriate use of skills or techniques. If it is due to lack of experience then the general guideline of: 'How would I feel if I were in his shoes?' would apply. This can be carried forward to the next interview on the basis of: 'I have never had this experi-ence and I would be grateful for your expertise since you have gone through it. Could you possibly tell me exactly how you felt and what it meant to you at the time?' In terms of inappropriate skills or techniques, this can best be described as a learning experience. This does not mean to say that the therapist can make excessive blunders or *faux pas*, but should mean that the ther-apist exhibits human frailties in respect of getting things wrong. This in itself can be used in therapy to re-enforce the one-down position and also to re-enforce the image that the therapist is not perfect but purely there to guide. Within nursing there appears to be a need to do the right thing all the time. When mistakes occur, then like history they cannot be re-written, but as long as the therapist learns from the experience there is no reason why she cannot use these mistakes within therapy. For example:

THERAPIST: Am I right in thinking that you and your wife want a divorce?

CLIENT: Absolutely not. I don't know where you got that idea from. We never said any such thing.

Rather than spend 15 minutes trying to justify to the client why you thought this was what he was saying, it is much easier to follow through with:

THERAPIST: I am sorry. I obviously misunderstood what you were saying. I didn't realise the amount of commitment that you and your wife have towards each other.

It frequently happens when following the general direction of the client's conversation, that the therapist concludes logically that the client's stated feelings have reached an impasse. However, it should be remembered that the client's verbal renderings to the therapist are only descriptive and not necessarily a fact of intent. In situations of domestic disharmony, whether between parents or parents and children, there are often angry words said in the heat of the moment. This does not mean that the words indicate intent; they may purely indicate the intensity of perception. Many therapists must see horrific domestic situations which seem to indicate that the clients involved wish to separate, without their actually saying so. However when separation is actually mentioned, the system closes ranks and the therapist ends up feeling thwarted. Unless there is blatant manipulation of the therapist, it is advisable for her to back down on the premise of a misunderstanding rather than continue to confront them with statements of: 'But you said...' The advantages of video recording equipment and/or team members who can observe therapy sessions in this area are immense as mistakes and misperceptions can be spotted, hopefully immediately, and therefore the consequences can be minimised. However the problems encountered by the community-based therapist can only be dealt with in hindsight. If the therapist is aware of the skills and techniques being used and is aware of the client's responses, then, remembering to 'test the water', the therapist should be able to minimise the consequences of any mistakes on the spot.

Another issue is the space allocated between therapy sessions. Each model of therapy has its own optimal time lapse. To a large degree the time lapse may be dictated by the therapist's case load or the availability of facilities. However the author believes that the time lapse between therapy sessions should be by mutual consent. Therapy cannot be geared towards allocation of rigid times. In general terms this model will work quite effectively with an initial period of one-week intervals and, at the discretion of the therapist and client, these can be dropped to two-, and then three- and if necessary four-week intervals. One-week intervals are suggested initially as clients frequently call the therapist again requesting clarification of what was said or the task set, usually within the first week. In such cases, re-enforcement of the tasks and clarification can be given with the promise of an early visit.

In some models of therapy the intervention or task is given at the close of the session. The rationale for this is that the clients cannot then say to the therapist: 'What do you mean?' as the therapist immediately disengages from the session. These therapists believe that if the client was given the opportunity to question the tasks, this would be a way of negating them. However this leads to what has been described as 'hand grenade therapy', that is, the therapist collects the information, assesses it, and delivers an intervention which would hopefully radically alter the system's method of functioning, withdrawing immediately. It should always be remembered that once a client or family enters into therapy, it is the therapist's responsibility to deal with that client and family when and as they require help. It is not sufficient to state that you only work from 9 a.m. to 5 p.m. and that you will only see the family on a monthly basis. This is gross irresponsibility and will probably engender a justifiable feeling of hostility from the client.

The information received by the therapist forms the baseline and springboard for the second and subsequent sessions and if the skills and techniques outlined have been employed then the therapist's options in term of directions and possible responses from the second session are of great advantage. The second session is vitally important and should be geared towards ascertaining whether or not the client has been able to achieve the tasks set. If they have been achieved, it can be assumed that the therapist is going in the right direction and avoiding the direction of previously attempted solutions. However if the client has been unable to achieve the desired tasks then the therapist must immediately question whether or not the tasks were too advanced in realistic terms, or whether there has been interference from other professionals or family members to sabotage the tasks. This again should be done by explicit questioning such as:

THERAPIST: I asked you to do ... Have you been able to do it?
CLIENT: No. I haven't been able to.

THERAPIST: How's that? Haven't you been able to allocate time to do it or did you find it too difficult? Of course, maybe you actually asked somebody in the family to help you with it. Could you tell me which family member you informed of the task I set you?

This method of questioning will identify whether there was a practical problem in completing the tasks or whether the client's motivation was not sufficient. More detailed examples of motivation enhancers will be described later.

Each session should be aimed at achieving momentum and direction towards the goals set. It is vitally important for the therapist to assess her own performance, as well as the client's, on a sessional basis, thus enhancing the opportunity of successful outcome.

Summary

This chapter has looked at the different types of formalised assessments as used by health visitors and district nurses in comparison to those used in psychiatry. Each assessment is designed to give the professionals the kind of information they require, sometimes to the exclusion of other pertinent information. It is essential to minimise analysing, interpreting or hypothesising as these skills rely on the therapist's expertise and experience. The Walker family were identified and it was described how they were subjected to the normal exposure of professionals entitled to be involved, without success. The common pitfalls of non-specific information were clearly identified. The use of genograms was illustrated. The skill of task-setting by using middle-line statements was exemplified. The importance of neutrality and validation was again emphasised in this area. Testing your ground as to the acceptability of tasks is a simple but very effective method of ensuring that time is not wasted in pursuing tasks which the client cannot or will not complete. The need to assess how other family members (present or absent) may respond to tasks set is vital to exclude undermining or sabotage. Motivation, at this stage, can be enhanced by indication of possible failure, a combination of the one-down position and normality. The need for therapy and therapist assessment is essential if treatment is to move fast and in the right direction. It is of prime importance to accept the client's perception and language not because it is 'the truth' or 'reality' but because it is his own. 'The most dangerous delusion of all is that there is only one reality. What there are, in fact, are many different versions of reality, some of which are contradictory, but all of which are the result of communication...' (Watzlawick, 1977).

Exercises

1 Try to identify which information in your current assessments is essential and which is secondary.
2 Which information do you pursue in subsequent sessions? Is it essential or secondary?
3 On your next session, be aware of any interpretations or suppositions you make. Did you check them with the client(s)?
4 Draw up genograms of your current cases. Do they make understanding clearer? Do they hold all essential information?
5 Practise making tasks which hold a middle line for all concerned. Take all viewpoints and find the common thread.
6 Do you assess your performance after each session? Plan the next session based on the outcome of the last session.

References

Baly, M. (1981). *The Mentally Ill. A New Approach to District Nursing*. Heinemann Medical, London, pp. 182–9.

Hua, E. K. (1974). Further meditations (6). In: *Kung Fu Meditations and Chinese Proverbial Wisdom*. Bantam Books, London.

Orr, J. (1985). Assessing individual and family health needs. In: Luker, K., Orr, J. (eds.) *Health Visiting*. Blackwell Scientific Publications, Oxford, pp. 101–20.

Watzlawick, P. (1977). *How Real is Real?* Vintage Books, New York, p. xi.

Further Reading

Barker, P. J. (1985) *Patient Assessment in Psychiatric Nursing*. Croom Helm, Beckenham.

6

Problems?

If the skills and techniques set out so far are followed, therapy will progress, although the speed of progression toward the goals will be proportional to expertise in using these skills. However, as everybody knows: 'It don't work out like that'.

There are of course clients who create problems for the therapist and if possible these problems should be avoided before they arise. However there are cases where this is either impossible or impractical.

There are three broad categories of clients who present as problems to the therapist. Firstly, the client who is referred to therapy against his will, under duress or under some form of threat if he does not comply. Secondly, the client who enters therapy with all good intentions and seems motivated toward achievement but as therapy progresses, his achievements become less and less to the extent that therapy does not work. Thirdly, the client who is always called away 5 minutes before the session is due to start or, for whatever reason, is never in attendance at sessions.

The client who enters therapy under duress is often referred into treatment by a third party, although it is not unknown for this type of client to refer himself. Examples of this type are: the child sent for treatment by his parents; the husband seeking help at the urging of his wife; the offender referred by probation services. The biggest mistake the therapist can make in this situation is to believe automatically that the client wishes therapy because he is present. It is therefore very important to check why the referred client is presenting for therapy. If it is assumed that the client is willing to enter therapy and elements of force or duress are not explored or elicited, then time may be wasted setting up tasks which the client will not do for a wide variety of imaginative reasons. Failure to identify this type of client initially will probably mean that he will then make all sorts of excuses as to why it is inconvenient to be seen. Common examples of this are the client wishing to have an appointment in the early or late evening; the client who frequently misses appointments and the client who deliberately generalises and fails to offer any specific definition of the problem. The client who is referred under duress is not necessarily the same as the customer who has no intention of buying. The client who has no intention of buying will probably never buy, whereas the client under duress can be brought into therapy by simple methods such as:

THERAPIST: If I'm reading this situation right, it seems that you don't particularly have any problems but your wife thinks you do. She thinks you drink too much. Is that right?

CLIENT: Yes, that's right. She seems to think that just because I spend Friday night with the boys having six or seven pints, I'm an alcoholic. She just doesn't seem to understand that I need time on my own.

THERAPIST: OK, I can accept that. What are the consequences of you going out for a drink? What is it about your wife's behaviour that you find hard to accept?

CLIENT: Well, she keeps on at me and she has indicated that unless I stop drinking, she will leave me.

At this stage in therapy it is relatively unimportant how much the client actually drinks. In fact it would be wrong to pursue the point at this time as it would justifiably lead the client to believe that the therapist is attempting to judge whether or not he has a problem. As stated, the client has clearly indicated that in his perception he does not have a problem with his drinking. However, a re-negotiated definition of a problem is emerging. The client is now stating that an area of his life in which he would like improvement is the interactions between his wife and himself. Treatment could therefore be initiated along the lines of:

THERAPIST: It seems to me that we would be wasting our time if we try to discuss your drinking habits. However it also seems to me that you do have a problem in that your wife is threatening to leave you unless she believes that you are either drinking less or at least attempting to cut down. Is there any way we could either convince your wife that you are attempting to solve her problem or at the very least is there anything we can do to get her off your back?

This opens up the way for therapy to commence on the client's own terms with something he sees as a problem. As the problematic interactions between this man and his wife revolve around the consequences of his drinking, the drinking can be indirectly treated without actually focusing on it. Another option open to the therapist for this type of client is to state:

THERAPIST: Well, it seems like a wasted journey but, as you are here, is there anything else that you would like to talk about? Is there any other area where maybe you do have a problem which does bother you?

Because the problem has been re-negotiated or identified differently it does not mean that the therapist is then tied down to solving just that problem. It is possible at some point for the therapist to bring in the issue of the original problem, that is, the drinking, as part of the treatment for 'getting his wife off his back'.

Another possible option would be for the therapist to say:

THERAPIST: It seems to me that it's your wife who is making an issue of this and I feel that I'd be wasting your time and mine if I continue to see you about this. Do you think your wife would be open to discussing it with me with a view to maybe getting her to be a bit more relaxed about your drinking?

If this tactic is acceptable to the husband, then his wife, who is the person actually complaining, can enter treatment, albeit on the assumption that she is giving background information to the therapist regarding her husband's drinking. Nonetheless, the therapist can very easily identify the interactions and behaviours between husband and wife which are promoting the problem and are identified as attempted solutions. As previously indicated, it is only a short step from here to setting a task for either or both of them in order to eliminate their negative interactions.

Another method of involving this type of client would be to use a paradoxical approach. This would involve actively advising the client against therapy. In the above example, the husband could be told that if he were to resolve what his wife considers to be the problem then she would probably find another behaviour with which to 'flog' him. In these circumstances it would be inadvisable to sort out the original problem as, by definition, he is at least relatively happy with being able to handle his wife via the drinking, whereas if the problem shifted to another behaviour, he might not be able to handle that as effectively.

If the client does not or will not consider any of these options then the best idea is to finish therapy there and then. However there are ways to end treatment therapeutically for this type of client. For example:

THERAPIST: It seems to me that you're saying you would like to enter therapy but I think we both realise that nothing would probably come of it. You obviously realise how important it is for your wife that you should be seen to enter therapy, even before you achieve anything. I would think the best thing to do is to find some other agency prepared to sit and talk to you without actually achieving anything. As that is not the way I work, I suggest that you try and find another agency. I'm sure you probably feel quite angry about this but I think I'm right and I'm sure that you will prove me right by being continually referred to different agencies.

This statement has a double effect of issuing a challenge which the client may or may not take up with the therapist. It also has an element of prediction and honesty. If he is aware that this is the case and wishes to continue seeking treatment, then at some point the message of this statement will hit home. If, on the other hand, he is unaware that this is happening, again at some future point the message will hit home and he may then be motivated to sit down and face facts.

Another difficulty which quite often occurs with clients referred under duress is what is termed the 'restrictive client'. This type of client is the one who consciously or unconsciously tries to thwart therapy by entering into collusion or coalition with the therapist. A relatively common example of this happened with the Walker family, mentioned in Chapter 5. Mary had taken an overdose following an attack on Jonathan earlier that morning while George was at work. As a result of the attack, the therapist had called round at the nursery to check Jonathan physically for marking or bruises and then called round at Mary's house. When the therapist arrive, George was home from work but in another room.

THERAPIST: I've seen Jonathan and he has some slight redness on his back. Because he was marked I have told your GP and have also told the nursery staff that if they are suspicious in the future then they should check Jonathan themselves.

MARY: Why did you go and tell them? You had no right to do that. I trusted you but now I know you are going to tell other people, I can't tell you things.

THERAPIST: It seems to me we have two different ideas of what I am supposed to be doing. As far as I'm aware, my job is somehow to improve the relationship between you and Jonathan to the satisfaction of you both. You appear to think I should be some sort of confidant. It would certainly help if you could trust me but you must realise that if I feel any information you give me is important enough to mention to anybody else, such as your doctor or social worker, then I must be at liberty to do so. You can believe me when I say I would only do that if I professionally believe that it is in your best interests.

MARY: How am I expected to get better if I can't trust people? It's bound to get worse now and for God's sake don't tell George what happened.

THERAPIST: If I am to help you at all, Mary, I must be free to make decisions in therapy which I think are best, otherwise you could just as easily be doing therapy on yourself without me.

At this George entered the room and commented on the silence:

GEORGE: What's happening?

THERAPIST: Mary has told me something which is significant and I believe you don't know of it. I've just been telling Mary that if therapy is to work, then there should be no secrets between any of us. So if you want to know what's been happening, Mary will tell you.

After some 5 minutes of continual questioning by George, Mary did tell him what had transpired that morning. Following an initial angry outburst, he became or appeared to become quite supportive and understanding.

It is best if this type of situation can be avoided beforehand by indicating to the client that a conspiracy of silence will not be entered into and should the client then not wish to make a revelation, it is entirely his responsibility. The other option, as shown above, is to be totally honest with those involved and indicate that something has been said in one person's absence which is significant but that it is up to the individuals concerned to communicate more openly with each other and it is not the therapist's responsibility.

Another form of restriction is when the client refuses to give permission for the therapist to see or speak to any other members of the family, despite it being apparent that their help would be beneficial. In such circumstances it would be unwise to force the issue by demanding approval or permission, but the client should be given the responsibility for making such a decision. For example:

THERAPIST: OK, it's obvious you don't want me to see your wife, so I have to respect your wishes despite the fact that I believe that therapy could progress much faster and probably less painfully for you if she were to be involved. We'll try to muddle along without her involvement.

This statement places the responsibility back on the client and also indicates that progress in therapy will now be slower as the result of his decision. As a re-enforcement, when the wife is mentioned in therapy, the therapist can state that without having met his wife, the information just given is of minimal value.

Another restrictive practice is intimidation through violence. Should violence or impending violence be indicated by the client's verbal or physical behaviour then the therapist will tend to tread very carefully in terms of the types of questions she asks. If this happens, therapy is obviously going to be a very slow and unproductive process. The client can readily see that touchy areas can best be dealt with by indicating potential violence. As a result he knows the therapist will withdraw or go off on a tangent from that particular subject, with the result that the client does not have to answer those questions. When clients indicate that they are quite prepared to use the potential of violence to avoid a certain line of questioning, the therapist can indicate that she is unable to deal with violence. For example, she can state to a client who is becoming aggressive: 'I can see you are obviously upset by this and I really would like to understand it better.

Could you tell me what is the best way to handle you when you begin to lose your temper? The clients response to the above question will give the therapist a clear indication of what she should do if the client begins to lose his temper. Another method of handling a violent client is to state: 'It is obviously good for you to express these intense feelings of emotion, although from my point of view, all that happens when people get aggressive around me is that I get anxious and paralysed. When that happens, I'm no use to anybody. So when people become violent the best thing for me to do is just to leave and forget about therapy.' Another method would be to use the one-down position. For example: 'When you indicate that you're getting aggressive, I just can't handle it. I can't think straight. If I can't think straight then I'm no use to you, so I would appreciate it if you could help me to help you by trying to control the anger despite how hard this would be for you.' It is impossible for violence to be the result and consequence of only one person's interactions. Violence is the result of an escalating process. For example:

WIFE: You never listen to me when I talk about my family.
HUSBAND: What do you mean, I never listen to you?
WIFE: See—you've not been listening to me just now.
HUSBAND: I would listen to you if you have something worth-while to say.
WIFE: Ah! Whatever I say doesn't count?'
HUSBAND: I'm going into the other room until you settle down.
WIFE: That's it. You always run away.
HUSBAND: I've had enough of you and your snide remarks. If you don't stop then I'll do something about it.

Another example of aggressive escalation is the arms race; one side invents one form of weapon more powerful than anything the other side has. Given time, the other side acquires the technology required and builds the same type of weapon, but more of them. The first side then builds newer stronger weapons, with the result that the other side also builds newer, stronger and more weapons. This process continues or can continue to the point of economic disaster for the countries involved.

Therefore if the challenge of superiority is not met by the therapist trying to enforce her own superiority, the interaction of the escalation suddenly becomes superfluous and inappropriate.

There is much talk in nursing circles regarding violence and potential violence and, in terms of the examples described above, which are basic systemic principles, it seems totally incomprehensible that the attempted solution in dealing with violence is to train all nurses in judo or karate. If this course of action was the solution to the problem of violence, then it would make more sense to short-cut the entire escalation process. Whilst it is admirable to be aware of violence, it is inappropriate to meet violence with such degrees of anxiety as to be paralysed by it. This will only serve to re-enforce the positive aspects of violence from the client's point of view. A somewhat serious and yet amusing anecdote in relation to violence is a situation in which the author was involved when called to deal with a man who was shooting at people with a rifle (fortunately missing) from his living-room window. On arrival the client turned the gun on the therapist, stating:

CLIENT: Who the hell are you? You're not another of those Communist pigs?
THERAPIST: Ah! You don't like them. Fine. How can you tell which ones are the Communists from here?
CLIENT: They're all bloody Communists.
THERAPIST: Do you know what? You would be able to shoot a lot more if you had somebody reloading that rifle for you.
CLIENT: Yes, I suppose I would.
THERAPIST: Why don't you let me reload because you seem like a genuine guy to me.
CLIENT: OK. Here you go—reload.

Whereupon the client threw the rifle to the therapist who then discarded it out of the room to other professionals. Although the client was angry at this response, the situation with the firearm had been averted. Within a matter of minutes the client was reassured that those present were there to help him and to try to resolve whatever problems he had.

The second type of client who creates problems in therapy is the one who fails to achieve any progress or fails to carry out identified tasks. As outlined in Chapter 5, failure to complete tasks usually indicates that one of two things has happened. Either the client and/or family have failed to understand what has been asked of them, a reflection on the therapist not having got the client's language or level of motivation correct, or the tasks may have been undermined by other family members who have more to lose than anticipated. In either instance it is important for the therapist to check whether the tasks have been completed. If they have not, the therapist must try and identify why the client and family have diverted their attention from the tasks set. It is again important to use simple, clear and direct questioning. For example:

THERAPIST: Have you been able to do as I asked?
CLIENT: No.
THERAPIST: That's unfortunate. Could you tell me what happened? Was it that you did not understand what I said or perhaps I set the tasks at a too difficult level?
CLIENT: Well, we actually started doing the task you set but my wife's parents came to stay with us for the weekend and they wondered why we were spending a quarter of an hour on our own rather than with them in the evenings. When we told them the reason, they said it was a waste of time because they had tried to do the same themselves and it was totally useless.

A situation has now arisen where outside influence is undermining the task set and the therapist now has two options. The first is to accept total responsibility for the failure and somehow re-motivate the family into following instructions. The second is to accept total responsibility for the failure and somehow block out the undermining effect of the in-laws. In the first instance the therapist's response could be:

THERAPIST: I am really sorry you were not able to complete the task, but it seems to me that I misjudged where you were at and what you were capable of. I admit that I probably misread the situation last time and that's why I asked you to do a task which was obviously too difficult. I can only say how sorry I am that I wasted the last week for you. I think maybe I am being a bit too keen. What I would suggest is we slow things down so that you have more time to form a solid base on which to build. At the end of this session, when we agree on what tasks to do, I think rather than give you a week, I should in fairness give you 3 weeks in which to complete them.

In this instance the therapist has used the 'go slow' theory as a motivation enhancer, which has the effect of speeding up therapy. If the client is genuinely and actively seeking the solution then the implicit message from the therapist is that by going slow, the solution becomes more distant. However if the client is in therapy for the sake of being in therapy rather than outcome, then again the go slow theory will activate the response that remaining in therapy requires some form of result.

In the second instance the therapist could respond by saying:

THERAPIST: I really am sorry that when we set the tasks last week, I didn't take into account the fact that your in-laws were visiting. In any case it would be unfair of me to ask you to keep your relatives away while you carry out the tasks. It seems to me that your in-laws are a very caring couple with your best interests at heart. Perhaps it would be unwise to disregard the obvious experience that they have in resolving problems, especially of the type that you as a family are encountering. What I would therefore like to suggest is that in order to make the best use of your in-laws, prior to making any decision in relation to your family, you actually ask their advice. For example, if the two of you think it would be a good idea to go to the cinema on a Friday night, give your in-laws a call on the Thursday to see whether they think it would be a good idea. That way you would be able to use their experience, knowledge and wisdom.

This example uses the fact that it has been positively identified that the couple in therapy listen to and in this case have acted on the advice of the in-laws. However the clients have now been given the option of either totally including the in-laws or excluding them from their discussions. The practical outcome of total inclusion would soon become apparent to the clients, as it would be impractical to ask for their advice on every matter. This in turn highlights the amount of influence the in-laws have on the clients. At some point the therapist could give hints as to how to work around this problem rather than confront it, by giving examples such as: 'The only time I ever have alone with my wife is either when everybody has gone to bed or when she is preparing a meal. So if I want to speak to her I go out to the kitchen and because it is a work area, we tend to be left alone. That's probably because if anybody else comes into the kitchen they might be asked to help out.' This should open up an awareness that there are times when they could be alone, although perhaps not in the formalised way they have envisaged.

Other situations where tasks have not been performed can be genuine and reasonable. For example, unexpected pressure at work which entails one or other partner having to work excessively long hours. In this instance it is recommended that rather than confront the issue of motivation, the therapist should use this pressure as being the greater of two evils. For example:

THERAPIST: I am sorry you were unable to complete the tasks and I appreciate the pressures that your work puts on you. I must admit that since you told me this my biggest worry is not really about the tasks, but how the increased pressure and stress of the work commitment might affect you or the situation. Like most things in life, if you divert your energies into one particular area then some other area of your life will probably pay the price.

This points out the realistic danger of excessive working, especially as it does reduce input by the spouse to whatever the problem area may be. It also points out that immersing oneself in work, possibly to avoid domestic problems, not only does not succeed, but also aggravates the original problem area. The client then has the option of stating that he will either decrease his work commitment or that therapy should perhaps be postponed for one or two weeks or longer.

Another method which minimises task failure is to predict failure or on occasions even to encourage failure. If there is any resistance to progress by the client or family, then this paradoxical effect will mean that in order to resist the therapist, the client or family must actually progress. The therapist can justify predictions of failure by stating that these are deliberately set to highlight the problem area, enabling everyone to gain greater understanding and awareness of the interactions leading up to and involved in the problem area. For example:

THERAPIST: I would like the two of you to try something over
   the next week. I'm not sure if you will be able to manage it.
   Thinking about it, it would possibly be best if you did try but
   didn't succeed. Yes, I want you both to set aside half an
   hour, no, make that three-quarters of an hour, to discuss
   how John's drinking affects you and for John to try to list
   what he feels are the reasons for his drinking. Tell each other
   how you feel. If you find this too much, and I think you will,
   then just record at which point you felt unable to continue.

The other aspect of this is that the therapist is using a spontaneous paradox, much like the client who is an insomniac and
deliberately attempts to get to sleep. By requesting that the
spontaneous behaviour, which is the problem, should be deliberately forecast and implemented then, like the insomniac attempting to sleep, it is impossible to achieve. The logical result is that
the problem behaviours or symptoms cease. If the behaviours or
symptoms do not cease, it can be logically pointed out that, as
they were consciously or deliberately thought of, then they must
be under conscious control.

The third type of clients who create problems for the therapist
is those who avoid attending therapy sessions. In the event of
non-attendance being logical and perhaps justifiable, any of the
above methods can be applied. However a greater problem for
the therapist is where non-attendance is a conscious or unconscious attempt to thwart therapy. Non-attendance, like failure to complete tasks set or clients referred under duress, is often
referred to by therapists as resistance to therapy. It is however the
author's belief that in order to be resistant, the client must have
something to resist against. It is therefore more positive and
constructive to look at what the client is resisting, rather than
why he is being resistant. The 'why' is purely the therapist's
perception of the client's non-compliance. The non-attender may
perhaps be threatened by the possible upset of the status quo
within the family or may see the therapist very much in the
one-up position. In the latter case the therapist should pursue the
one-down position, albeit in that individual's absence. Again this
can be pursued directly or indirectly. For example:

THERAPIST: (*father absent*) I'm sure that (father) would like to
   be present but I can understand his reasons for not being

here tonight. He obviously knows this family a lot better than I do or ever will and, in the light of his non-attendance, I can only surmise that he is either protecting the family as he sees fit or he may be protecting himself. I don't know which of these it may be and in fact it may not be either. Nonetheless, I think we should proceed as if he were here.

This statement ascribes power to the absent member and openly recognises this. It also makes it clear that the absent member is absent for positive and logical reasons. By the therapist's admission that the absent member has more knowledge and a greater commitment to the family unit, it is quite possible that if this information is relayed to the absentee he will feel less anxious, less threatened and more liable to come into therapy for future sessions. A less direct and more implicit approach would be for the therapist to attribute a behaviour of quality to the absent member which the therapist believes he does not have. For example:

THERAPIST: I am sure if your father were here he would state that he totally understood that particular situation and would act accordingly.

MOTHER: No, he wouldn't. He would come down on Tommy (son) like a ton of bricks.

THERAPIST: I'm sorry, but the impression I get of your husband is that he would be completely understanding and would be the last person on earth to use discipline.

If this conversation continues, the therapist can state:

THERAPIST: Well, no matter. Your husband isn't here. Let's continue.

If this process is continued throughout therapy then the family will get the impression that the therapist is misperceiving the attributes and attitudes of the absent member and they in turn will try and exert family pressure on him to attend the next session. It may be that in the information relayed back to the absent member, a challenge has also been set down by the therapist, especially if such phrases are interspersed, such as: 'Well, if he were here he could speak for himself' or: 'It's a shame he's not here to answer for himself.' It is possible that the absent member, in this case the father, will make a point of attending the next session if for no other reason than to confirm or deny the attributes the therapist has given him. It is important at this point that the therapist should not give an attribute to an absent member without leaving the option of: 'Of course, I could be wrong.' When the absent member attends in future, the therapist can then quite easily state: 'Well, what I actually said was that I thought you might have this quality but I did also state that I could be wrong.' The therapist is then employing the one-down position, avoiding confrontation and at the same time has the previously absent member present. Therefore, by attributing either extreme positive or negative qualities to the absent member, the only response that he can take is to attend the following sessions.

There are of course situations where non-attendance is therapeutic. Some family therapists believe that family therapy is not family therapy unless all members are present. Some go as far as to make this rule a precondition of therapy. The author believes that family therapy is a concept and a collection of specific skills and techniques which, when employed on any number of family members, will be successful in initiating family change, whether perceptual or, as a result, behavioural. There are occasions when key members of the family or even the identified client need not be present in order for family therapy to work. In the Walker family case (Chapter 5) there was an occasion when Mary failed to attend. Her husband made allegations regarding the intensity and number of attacks by her on Jonathan. This session was spent getting George to look at the overall situation with a different perception. The result was that George no longer regarded his wife as a failure but rather as a person who did not completely control certain situations. It was suggested that George should try to identify these situations and then help his wife. It soon became apparent that by altering George's perception of the situation he was able to see Mary's behaviour in a different light and his own behaviour subsequently altered. He offered a better quality of support instead of the negative harassment he had previously displayed. This example shows that although Mary and Jonathan had the problem, the situation actually improved by therapy with George.

Another example is an instance where a 10-year-old child was not attending school. The child was in fact never seen by the therapist. The therapist saw the parents alone and established the pattern of interactions which led up to non-attendance at school. The parents were then given tasks which re-focused their attention away from the child. This resulted in the child re-commencing attendance at school. The child had been using defiance of parental authority as a means of gaining attention. It is quite possible that the child had not been attending school due to a relationship problem at school. However once the pattern of the parents' interactions had been established in relation to the child attending school it became evident that the interactional problem, which may have been carried over to the school setting, was in fact initiated at home. Therefore the avenue of interactions at school was not pursued.

It is evident that an individual's perception of a problem will dictate his behaviour in attempting or achieving a solution for that problem. As the client experiences failure of attempted solutions, pessimism creeps in and he will then perhaps paint the picture blacker than it is. As pessimism increases, motivation decreases. Therefore an invaluable skill that the therapist can and should use at any point in therapy is re-framing. Re-framing is commonly used by most people when telling jokes. The principle of a joke is that the listener is led to believe in a concrete, logical framework and the essence is the punchline which completely throws the framework out by introducing another, less obvious framework. The punchline is the realisation that, although you may have been thinking along a logical line, you were in fact following the wrong line. This is re-framing.

In the Walker family case re-framing was used to shift George's perception of the problem away from the negative aspect of child battering to a more positive one of over-disciplining.

The author uses re-framing especially where the perception is one of medical diagnostics, which may hold negative values due to the association of illness and lack of control. For example, the following are common usages of re-framing. It must be remembered that reframing should be used with appropriate sincerity and seriousness and not flippantly or derisively.

CLIENT: My husband is an alcoholic.
THERAPIST: You mean he drinks too much.
CLIENT: My wife is obsessional.

THERAPIST: You mean she's over-zealous about...

CLIENT: My wife's a manic–depressive.

THERAPIST: You mean she has ups and downs but to the extreme.

CLIENT: My husband is hostile and aggressive.

THERAPIST: You mean he doesn't appreciate or listen to your viewpoint but is committed to his own.

CLIENT: My son is schizophrenic.

THERAPIST: You mean he cannot communicate clearly or properly.

CLIENT: My husband is impotent.

THERAPIST: You mean your husband does not reach orgasm.

The list of possible re-framing is endless. In essence the therapist tries to direct the client's perception away from negative aspects and connotations of certain words towards a more positive and, in therapy terms, more workable definition of the problem.

Many of the above instances of re-framing also include a degree of normalisation. This entails re-defining the problem in terms of normal behaviour, again moving away from the negative aspects of diagnostic and models. As described in the Walker case, it may take some time before the client accepts the re-definition. On occasions, if the therapist continually slips the re-frame into conversation throughout the session, then by the end of the session, the client should accept the re-definition. For example, when working with an alcoholic, it would be inconceivable to the spouse or family to focus attention on the interactions around the drinking unless the re-frame has been made explicit. In this case, the repercussions of not making the re-frame explicit would be that the family is unable to follow the train of thought logically. They may justifiably feel that, due to the interactional method of questioning, they are partly responsible or to blame for the client's drinking, whereas once the re-frame has been made explicit, then the therapist's line of questioning falls within the logic of that re-frame. The above example is based on the principle that: 'Nobody is to blame—everybody is responsible'. Blame is a process whereby the person pointing the finger can dissociate himself and thereby free himself from any form of guilt. On the other hand, responsibility can be shared and make problems and illnesses more workable.

The above are examples of positive re-framing, which make the identified problem more amenable to practical solutions and practical working. There is also the skill of negative re-framing, which, although the reverse of positive re-framing, has much deeper implications in the relationship between client and therapist. An example of negative re-frame would be:

CLIENT: I am overweight.
THERAPIST: It seems to me that you are underestimating it. I would say you were obese.

Obviously it would be a gross insult to make this statement under normal circumstances. It is therefore important that the relationship between client and therapist should be clearly identified before using negative re-framing. The therapist must be sure that although the client may feel hurt, he certainly does not feel rejected or insulted. There is a subtle difference. Not only is a close relationship with the client a precondition to using this skill but so is the fact that therapy has not been achieving the desired results. Negative re-framing can be used to enhance motivation and achieve results, especially where the therapist is indicating either long-term therapy or no solution therapy. The author recalls a case where a female client was being seen over a period of six months with a view to reducing her weight so that she would be acceptable to the anaesthetist for general surgery. Because she was overweight, the operation could not be performed and as she was in pain she had no motivation to lose weight. In other words there was a vicious circle which promoted negative behaviours. After some months of attempting all forms of positive interventions with no result, the author decided to use negative re-framing. The initial conversation went as follows:

THERAPIST: It seems to me that we are not really getting any-where in terms of weight loss, despite all your efforts to follow the tasks I set.
CLIENT: It's not your fault. I just don't seem able to lose weight. I think maybe I will just have to settle for being well built.
THERAPIST: I hope you don't take offence at this but in the light of the fact that you are not responding to my evaluation of things, which may be wrong, then it seems to me we might as well be honest with each other. I do not think that your

obesity and general lack of hygiene will actually improve, especially within the next three months. I accept responsibility for not providing the appropriate therapy. I am sorry about this but some people remain obese for some period of time and then suddenly for no reason begin to lose weight. Perhaps you are one of these people. All I can hope for now is that at some point in the future you will suddenly lose your fat and become less obese, less gross. I would imagine that if that were to happen, then your personal hygiene would also improve. However I do realise that I have not been able to help you and that is why I think we should be honest with each other.

The client's immediate response was to defend the therapist, although she was hurt that the therapist had been so blunt. This was followed through by the therapist stating that honesty should be the best policy. The client was seen approximately one month later and she joyfully reported that she had lost approximately half a stone in weight. The therapist remained negative rather than falling into the trap of congratulating the client. This procedure was used for the following three months until the client stated that she was down to her operation weight. The trap of congratulating the client following negative re-framing is that as soon as positive rewards are brought into play, the client then has the option of reverting to the previous behaviours, whereas if the negative cycle is maintained, the client will continue to respond in the desired manner. Even on discharge, this client continually asked for reassurance and praise but the therapist left the client with the statement:

THERAPIST: I accept that you've done it but I don't know how. I'm sure you are bound to put the weight back on within the next week.

The therapist must be sure of the situation and the relationship before even considering the use of negative re-framing.

Negative re-framing may seem very similar to paradoxical intervention. The author believes that paradox should be left to those who firmly believe in its value and feel perfectly safe in its use. The Milan group have long been using the paradoxical approach, although in the foreword of their book Dr Stierlin states that: 'The authors have been working as a team for approximately eight years' (Palazzoli *et al.*, 1978). The principle of paradox is to use the resistance shown by individuals or families in response to therapy suggestions or tasks. The individual or family is asked to follow certain instructions in the belief that because they are resistant, they will follow a different line. From the author's experience it cannot be emphasised enough that there is a lot more to the process of paradox than purely desiring the client to do the opposite of what is stated. The author knows of an incident involving the use of paradox which went as follows. A client was expressing feelings of worthlessness and did not seem to be responding to therapy. He was asked to respond in future by not asking for help but following his own inclinations. The unfortunate result was suicide, an option for the client which the therapist had failed to take into consideration. Paradox is for those who feel safe using it. The author believes it is more constructive and therapeutic to eliminate resistance by altering the *therapist's* position rather than the *client's*. Resistance is a response by the client to what appears to him to be an illogical request. If the therapist continues to have difficulty in helping the client or family achieve progress, it may be that although information is concrete and precise, the family is in collusion against the therapist. That is: 'I will give no information which may be used against me'. In such cases a different method of collecting information may be required, that is, by circularity. Circularity involves no direct questioning of an individual of his own behaviour but third-party questioning. For example:

THERAPIST: (*to son*) What does your father do when your mother raises her voice?

SON: He gets up and shouts at her.

THERAPIST: (*to mother*) What does your son do when your husband starts raising his voice?

MOTHER: He leaves the room. He knows there's going to be an argument.

THERAPIST: (*to father*) What does your wife do when your son leaves the room?

FATHER: She tells me that it's all my fault.

Without circularity this clear picture could have been presented thus:

THERAPIST: (*to father*) What do you do when your wife raises her voice?

FATHER: I get angry.

THERAPIST: (*to son*) What do you do?

SON: I've usually left by then, but I can hear them arguing.

THERAPIST: (*to mother*) What do you do?

MOTHER: When he gets really angry I point out how destructive that is.

The second example is less clear and more confusing in terms of sequence and pattern. This is because each person is defending his own behaviour as correct, logical and not intended to be threatening or challenging. In the first example the son can be as open as he wants as his behaviour is not in question. Likewise, mother about father and son, and father about mother and son.

Humour can also motivate. Those who attend dental surgeries or have children who attend, can bear witness to the relaxing effect humour can have. I know of no therapist who denies the importance or place of humour in therapy. The essence is that the humour should be appropriate and heart-felt. The author recalls an incident when a 'depressed' client was referred to him. The client had been banned from driving as a result of a bald tyre (at that time a third endorsement meant an automatic ban); his wife could not drive, his place of work was 8 miles away and public transport was non-existent. He was having an extension built to his house which had been built to the wrong plans and had to be demolished. There was a large hole where the back wall used to be and his neighbours were suing him as a result of structural damage to their house when the builders demolished his wall. It was mid-winter and his two daughters had measles. And he was depressed! When informed that even if he contemplated suicide, with his luck he would fail (said with a smile, not a laugh), the client burst into laughter and said: 'Yes, it can only get better.' Being too serious can be a hindrance to therapy. On occasions, being able to laugh at your own responses and those of the client makes therapy easier. You become more humanistic and perhaps more importantly, therapy becomes more than a business, it becomes enjoyable for both client and therapist.

Summary

In this chapter the types of clients who are most liable not to respond or to become involved in therapy were discussed. Specific problem areas were being referred under duress, failure to respond or achieve, and non-attendance. The possible causes of and solution to client resistance were also explored, together with methods of enhancing motivation. The use of positive and negative re-framing were exemplified with the criteria for their use. The importance of judgement on the client–therapist relationship was highlighted, especially where paradox is concerned. Lack of progress was dealt with in terms of motivation, the therapist not using the client's language and also the use of circularity and humour.

This chapter identified the skills and techniques for dealing with certain situations and the need to be very sure and specific about what is happening before using such skills.

Exercises

1 If you are experiencing problems or lack of progress, do you ask yourself: 'What am I doing wrong?' rather than make the blasé comment: 'They're difficult'?
2 Try to identify exactly where you are going wrong and if necessary ask the client or family for advice. (Re-enforcement of the one-down position.)
3 Make a list from your current case load of the diagnostic terms used and attempt to re-frame them positively. Present the re-frame to the client and monitor the response.
4 Try to use circularity the next time you have two or more family members present.
5 If something is genuinely funny, tentatively share it with the client and if the response is good, notice the more relaxed atmosphere.

Reference

Palazzoli, M. S., Boscolo, L., Cecchin, G., Prata, G. (1978). *Paradox and Counterparadox*. London, Jason Aronson, p. vii.

Further Reading

MacPhail, W. D. (1986). Skills in family therapy. *Nursing Times*; 82:26:49–51.

7

Difficult Areas

M any nurses perceive certain areas of psychiatry and psychiatric illness as special, with their own special inherent
problems. As indicated previously within this model, if the therapist believes a particular area holds inherent special problems,
then problems and difficulties will certainly arise.

A re-enforcement of this is the common practice of community
services of appointing nurses to specialist positions. For example,
community psychiatric nurse with responsibility to: the elderly;
drug abuse; alcohol abuse; child and adolescent psychiatry and
behavioural therapist.

Some believe the emergence of specialist nurses is due to recognition of the fact that the field of general psychiatry is too wide
and varied for a generalised training programme to equip the
nurse to cover all of the areas adequately. Some believe the
creation of specialist fields is a political expediency in response to
society's statements that things are out of control in particular
fields. Others believe there should not be specialist areas but that
a more in-depth, intensive training should be undertaken as part
of basic training. This would avoid the accusation of élitism.
However at the moment it cannot be denied that many community psychiatric nurses believe there are specialist areas with
inherent specific problems.

It is therefore the purpose of this chapter to look at some
specific areas and offer a formulation of how this eclectic model
of therapy would deal with them. The areas studied will be:
sexual problems, drug and alcohol abuse, children and adolescents, psychotic clients and ethnic minorities.

Sexual Problems

For the purpose of this chapter, sexual problems are defined into
three main categories: child sex abuse (including incest), adult
sex abuse or rape, and sexual dysfunction.

Child Sex Abuse (Including Incest)

Burnham (1986) does not mention the causation or treatment of incest other than that it 'would be viewed in hierarchical terms as breaking the appropriate sexual boundary'. Sugden *et al.* (1986) give one paragraph defining paedophilia. Minde *et al.* (1986) do not mention abuse or incest at all, neither does Barker (1986). This may indicate that child sex abuse is seen as a specialist area and therefore not part of family therapy or within the role of the psychiatric nurse. This may be partially true as, when incest does occur, there is a legal compulsion for statutory bodies to become involved, that is, social services, NSPCC and the police.

Incest is generally defined as sexual intercourse between two people who are prohibited from marriage by law due to blood relationship. It is generally believed that the number of incest cases which come to light are the tip of the iceberg, perhaps because children relate adults to incidents which they do not like to hear and therefore assume the child is lying. Children do not generally lie in this situation, as they do not have in-depth awareness of the manipulative powers of not telling the truth. They sometimes exaggerate in terms of self-protection, such as: 'If I say I've done it, then you will not hit me'. It is perhaps paradoxical that adults are considered innocent until proven guilty, whereas on such occasions children are considered to be lying until proven honest.

There are some interesting statistics available on child sexual abuse. As a general indication of the level of the problem: 'one in four girls and one in 10 boys will be sexually molested before the age of 18' and 'the typical incest relationship is initiated between the ages of five and seven and lasts a minimum of two years before it is discovered' (Friesen, 1985). As a result, the vast majority of incest cases will only become apparent some time after the process has been initiated and become established.

This is somewhat different from adult sex abuse or rape, which usually has only existed for a short time before being reported. Although a basic sensitive approach of caring towards the victim remains relatively the same, the psychological impact of the trauma may vary greatly because of the duration of the process.

Incest or child sex abuse is usually initiated at a prepubertal stage. It could be argued that it is a result of a poor marital relationship. However it should be recognised that children do get into situations which they cannot control or escape from. There are many theories on the initiation and continuance of incest. One theory is that of 'the seductive daughter', when the daughter is learning to use her own sexuality, usually with a safe parent, that is the father. The father's response is that of an adult male towards a seductive female. However: 'It is the adult's responsibility to assess the short-term and long-term potential harm and not to throw better judgement to the wind and sexually exploit the child' (Friesen, 1985). Another theory is that the mother assists by turning a blind eye to the daughter's naive sexual advances towards the father. However: 'Many incestuous fathers are having an active sex life with their wives and at the same time exploiting their daughters' (Friesen, 1985). There is however a theory with which most authors on the subject agree: the theory of the conspiracy of silence. The child's silence is usually obtained by threats of: 'If you tell, Daddy will go away for a long long time and you will not see him again.'

Another interesting dynamic of incest and general child sex abuse is identification with the aggressor. The victim can logically conclude: 'My life is in his hands. Therefore as long as I live, he is protecting me. If this protection stops, then my existence may be in danger. Therefore I submit. If I submit, then he has the power to return.' The process may therefore go on for some time without any family member becoming suspicious and without the victim ever being able to come forward and tell her story.

As with all other psychiatric illnesses and processes, there can be classified predisposing factors and symptoms, some of which are included below. These were identified during a workshop on sexually traumatised adults, children and adolescents conducted by Louis and Diana Everstine (1977) at the Mental Research Institute.

Factors

1 These children tend to be scapegoats and isolated from other family members.
2 They can be the children of mothers who work late or all day and fathers who are at home for whatever reason.
3 Concern should be aroused on the part of the therapist when a child is described as: 'Daddy's little girl' or 'nothing but a dirty little whore'.

4 Either of the parents may have been sex abuse victims themselves.
5 The child may have a pseudomaturity towards sex.
6 The child may physically go through the motions of imitating sex or grabbing other people's sexual organs.
7 The child may actually run away whenever any close relationship is building up.

Symptoms

These can include:
1 Phobias.
2 Bed-wetting.
3 Temper tantrums.
4 A change in toilet behaviour.
5 Parental exclusion of caring.
6 Extreme changes in normal habits.
7 Genital pain.

It is fortunate that we have a legal system which protects children from known abuse. On the other hand, it is unfortunate that this legal system tends to exclude any form of treatment or method of dealing with this syndrome other than compulsory separation. However there does now seem to be a trend towards obtaining psychotherapeutic help for such families.

It is distressing but true that such problems do exist within society. The above symptoms are indications of cases where abuse may be occurring but they are not diagnostic on their own. The legal problem, or one of them, is that such symptoms can be seen as diagnostic because of their concrete nature, but this can be erroneous. In the light of recent events within Britain, i.e. at Cleveland, it has become clear that the present methods or interpretation of methods of dealing with child sex abuse are far from satisfactory. What is essential is that professionals must work in conjunction with each other and not as solitary agents.

Adult Sex Abuse or Rape

The main difference between child sex abuse and adult rape tends to be that the former occurs over a long period of time and the latter occurs suddenly. Due to maturity in terms of life experience, the adult process tends to fall into the process of psycho-social transition. The immediate response is one of denial, followed by the guilt process of 'why me?' and 'if only'. When wondering 'why me?' the victim will blame herself for being available, being in that place etc., whereas in reality there is no implication that the victim brought the incident on herself. While thinking 'if only' the victim will believe that if only she had dressed differently, if only she had avoided certain areas, the incident would not have occurred.

One of the major psychological aspects in reaction to rape in adults is that they will try to prevent a spontaneous parental response. They believe that if they disclose the facts to their parents, the parents will respond in terms of: 'It serves you right' or 'What did you do to encourage him?'

In terms of psychological responses adult and child victims tend to follow a pattern of disorientation, disorganisation, confusion and shock for up to approximately one month. This is because they have been forced to confront a life-or-death situation, especially so for the adult where the threat generally is: 'If you do not do as I say, I will kill you.' The victim is therefore confronted with the question of survival. It is perhaps interesting to note that her response tends to be: 'I nearly died' or 'I was violated' whereas the social response tends to be: 'What exactly happened?' The beliefs, relationships and trust in others of the rape victim have been assaulted and there is therefore a permanent change in these criteria. The result is that her self-assertion will diminish greatly and she will find minor sexual confrontations extremely difficult to deal with.

Like child abuse, it is surmised that many rape cases never come to light due to the fact that the process of dealing with these cases comes under the legal system, making it necessary for the victim to re-live the traumatic event. Many victims do not feel able or willing to undergo this ordeal. Consequently many do not report the incident or do report it but are unable to attend the court appearance. If therapeutic intervention is not available, then the state of shock will often fade into depression with possible resultant symptoms, such as sleep disorders, food disorders, distorted body image or fear of sexuality. Due to the shock effect and the level of others' comprehension of these symptoms, these factors alone could lead to further assaults. Under existing criminal law, many victims find that it is not a case of the aggressor being proven guilty but rather the credibility of the victim's sexuality that is in question. Whether or not the act was against the victim's will is often questioned in court.

Treatment and therapy for child and adult sex abuse

The initial response from the community agency must be twofold to achieve the ultimate therapeutic aim, helping the client with both the legal and the emotional process.

From the legal aspect it is important to find out how many hours ago the rape took place. If it was within a few hours, a medical examination should be encouraged to gain physical evidence. The police should be involved as soon as possible and if necessary the therapist should remain with the client to give emotional support during the interview. The therapist should make the first visit as soon as possible. If the victim has a supportive family who are aware of the situation, the therapist should be aware that they may feel they have failed in their role as protector and should recognise the pain they are consequently experiencing. It is also important to remember that some victims may want to be held physically, whereas others do not. Victims of rape usually insist that they no longer feel they have a sense of control over their lives. Again it is important to ascertain whether or not this is the experience of the individual victim. If the therapist tiptoes around the factual basis of the trauma, this may be seen as a silencing response and can lead the victim to think that the therapist does not care.

As in any major psychosocial transition, certain responses are normal, that is, depression, guilt, anger, anxiety and phobia. It is essential to reassure the client that these emotions are a normal process, that the victim is normal with normal responses although the trauma is not a normal event.

In physical trauma there is visible evidence of the traumatic event, for example, a broken arm or leg. However in the case of incest or rape, the psychological traumas of violation and loss of faith or trust are not visible.

The therapist should remember to accept and validate the client's statements in terms of what she had to do to survive and whatever graphic details she may use in relating the incident.

Many victims will refuse medication, especially tranquillisers, as they want to be in control. If this is the case, the phenomenon of flashbacks should be explained to them. Flashbacks are a re-living of the initial traumatic situation due to logical subliminal stimuli, which may be something the aggressor said, a certain smell, or certain sounds in the background which seemed significant at the time.

It is also helpful to ask the victim to write down everything she can remember and put it in an envelope. She should do this for several days, irrespective of whether or not she is aware that what she is writing on the third day disagrees with what she wrote on the first day. This helps her express emotions felt at the time and may also yield information which could assist the police.

There is no fixed duration of therapy in such cases. Depending on the individual's progress, therapy can last from months to years. In many cases the depression following rape will turn to overt anger if the aggressor is caught and brought to trial. As stated previously, the problem here is that the victim must re-live the attack in court in front of the aggressor as well as submitting to the more inhumane aspect of the proceedings by having her own sexuality questioned. However in Britain movements are beginning to be made towards allowing video tape recordings of statements or interviews with the victim as evidence in court.

Therefore the main goals of treatment for both the child abuse victim and the rape victim are similar. Both should be encouraged to regain control of their lives by simple task-setting. Both should be validated by informing them that their responses are perfectly normal although the situation was abnormal. Both should be encouraged to express their emotions. In both instances, therapy may be long-term but, in view of the nature of the trauma, the therapist should be prepared to commit herself to such a duration.

Sexual Dysfunction

The third and perhaps most commonly encountered (as opposed to most common) sexual problem is sexual dysfunction. The main causations of sexual dysfunction are broadly categorised into two areas: physical and psychological.

There are many physical causes which may decrease libido, produce impotence, impair erection or arousal, impair responsiveness and the ability to reach orgasm in both males and females. These are adequately defined by Kaplan (1978) and come under the headings of general ill health and chronic painful illness, liver diseases, endocrine disorders, local genital diseases, surgical conditions, neurological disorders and vascular disease. These physical causes range from urethritis to temporal lobe tumour.

There are other causes of sexual dysfunction and perhaps especially important in the psychiatric field is the influence of drugs on sexual functioning. Common categories of drugs that can cause sexual dysfunction are: anti-hypertensive agents, anti-psychotic drugs and tricyclic anti-depressants, as well as central nervous depressants, such as sedatives and anxiolytics. Under this last category also comes such drugs as cannabis, alcohol, methadone and heroin (*Medical Letter*, 1983). When a client is referred with sexual dysfunction it is important to examine and eliminate the possibility of physical causation before considering psychological causations. It is quite possible that although the causation is physical, the client may require some form of short-term therapy. This could be supportive or normalising. For example, the therapist could explain that it would appear that the loss of sexual function is not within his physical or psychological control due to the probable influence of the drugs he is taking. Discussion with the prescribing agency should then take place regarding assessment of the risks of cutting down the drug in question or even withdrawing it altogether. If a reduction is not possible and the client does not respond to simple tasks, then therapy should perhaps be geared initially towards his acceptance of his reduced sexual functioning.

The second category of sexual dysfunction is that of the psychological. There are three main categories under this heading: lack of arousal, lack of penetration or of ability to allow penetration and lack of satisfactory conclusion.

Lack of arousal is usually due to a failure to communicate either circumstantial needs or emotional or physical needs. For example, in cases where a couple rigidly adheres to a programme of sex, if the circumstances change but this is not communicated to the other person, a vicious circle of behaviours may ensure. For example, a businessman indicates by his previous behaviour that he is available for sexual intercourse on Tuesdays, Thursdays and the weekends. Suddenly the day of his business meetings changes to Thursdays which necessitates working extra hours. On his return home he is excessively physically tired but does not communicate this to his partner. Problems then occur in terms of arousal as the man is unable to obtain an erection due to physical fatigue. His partner is not able to understand the reason for this as she has not been told of his changed routine and her immediate reaction will be to feel rejected. The commonly employed attempted solution will be to try harder and his partner will attempt to become more seductive. When the man still fails to respond, not only does his partner experience a re-enforcement of rejection, but he will begin to experience guilt for failing to respond. The simplest method of treatment is for the man to communicate the change in circumstances to his partner and for the couple to re-arrange their sexual timetable.

There are times when neither partner will want to have sexual intercourse for whatever reasons. There are also times when, although not particularly wanting sexual intercourse, it takes place if one partner is aroused by the other. There are also obviously times when both partners actively wish sexual intercourse to take place. It is important to point out to clients that, to have successful, enjoyable intercourse, they must inform each other which of these categories they belong to at any particular time.

It is quite possible for one partner to become bored with the rigidity of the sexual programme, either in terms of frequency of occurrence or circumstances. For example, the woman may not always enjoy the missionary position, that is, with the woman submissive. She may prefer on occasions to enjoy the woman dominant position. The man may prefer his partner to initiate sexual contact. Either may prefer sexual intercourse to take place somewhere other than the bedroom. Perhaps what used to be pleasurable no longer holds the same level of pleasure. New methods of pleasurable stimuli should therefore be sought.

The simplest method of re-instating the arousal process is for both partners to renegotiate their patterns of sexual activity, for example, the time and location. Sexual activity need not only take place in the evening, in bed. It is accepted that when the couple have children, their options are obviously reduced. Nonetheless, with a little imagination there is no reason why alternative patterns of sexual activity cannot take place. Another method of re-instating arousal can be to ask both partners to be aware of the physical sensations they experience when soaping themselves with their hands (not a flannel) the next time they have a bath or shower. As pleasurable sensations do not just come from the genital areas, this task will focus on the varying areas which cause pleasant sensations. This can then be re-enforced by asking the couple to soap each other and at the same time, communicate these sensations to each other. Couples should be encouraged to try new experiences with each other on the proviso that if one partner finds it displeasurable, that activity should cease immediately. Such activities could include mutual masturbation, oral sex or penile or breast stimulation. It may be that lack of arousal is due to an insufficient amount of stimulation either in terms of pressure or in terms of time. It is not unknown for some men to believe that because they are ready for penetration then the woman should also be ready. This is not so. Some men do not touch their partners' breasts; some do not even kiss their partners or express their feelings during intercourse.

It is therefore important to establish a specific pattern of verbal and non-verbal behaviours in the arousal process so that alternative suggestions can be offered. Masters and Johnson (1966) provide recommended reading in terms of human sexual responses during the stages of arousal and intercourse.

Lack of penetration, impotence or erectile dysfunction does not indicate absence of arousal for the man in psychological terms, but means that for some reason the penis fails to become erect. This is usually due to anxiety in relation to the sexual act, either in terms of premature ejaculation or the belief that there will not be a satisfactory conclusion. As a result, it is quite common for the man to develop depression together with the initial anxiety. This problem is often the result of a previous negative or unsuccessful experience. By failing to gain an erection, a repeat performance of a previous disaster can then be avoided.

A common method of dealing with this problem is to prohibit sexual intercourse —that is, penetration—until further notice, as well as instructing the couple to follow tasks of identifying pleasurable areas of their own and their partner's body. There are two aspects to this task. The first is that the client is asked to concentrate on the pleasurable aspects of touching, say, the genitalia or having them touched without actually being requested to indulge in any form of performance. This reduces anxiety. The second aspect is that the more pleasure the client obtains, the less liable he is to worry about his performance and, by requesting that no sexual intercourse takes place, the anxiety disappears. If the client's partner is also present when the task is being set, she will realise that she cannot make any justifiable claims in relation to her partner's performance either verbally or non-verbally.

For the female, the lack of ability to allow penetration is usually due to either vaginismus or frigidity. Vaginismus involves the muscles around the vagina contracting so tightly that penetration becomes impossible. Frigidity is the lack of physical and emotional responses to sexual stimulation or intercourse. In either instance the task set would be the same as for lack of arousal. The client would be requested to get to know her own body with her own hands in terms of physical feelings. When she felt comfortable with this, she would then be asked to get comfortable with the pleasurable experiences of her partner's hands on her body. However, with vaginismus and frigidity, an extra task would be introduced: a programme of vaginal penetration ranging from small-diameter objects to the penis. It is usually more therapeutic for the partner to be present when these tasks are being undertaken by the woman, although there may be occasions when she will prefer to be alone.

The third area of unsatisfactory conclusion is usually the result of premature ejaculation or non-orgasm. In these cases the exact specific behaviour during the arousal period and intercourse should be explored. For premature ejaculation, one of two methods may be employed. The first is the Semans procedure (Kaplan, 1978) which requires the man to signal to the woman to stop manual stimulation of the penis as he feels his orgasm approaching and to repeat this procedure until his control is obtained. The other method would be dependent on the man's recovery cycle. If he has a fast recovery rate to erection, there is no reason why he cannot first ejaculate during the arousal period. His ejaculatory response will then be slowed down and once he obtains an erect penis again, penetration can take place. In the event of retarded ejaculation or a slow recovery rate, the couple could be advised to extend their arousal period before penetration to accommodate this.

During all forms of sex therapy, the therapist should remember that there are myths regarding sexual performance and where appropriate she should dispel these myths. Examples of these are: that women must have an orgasm in order to enjoy sexual intercourse; men must ejaculate to enjoy sexual intercourse; men and women should always have simultaneous orgasms.

There are many positions for enjoying sexual intercourse. If penetration is a problem, there is no reason why the couple cannot be advised to experiment with a variety of positions with either male or female being dominant.

Drug and Alcohol Abuse

Drugs and alcohol have been used by varying cultures virtually since time began, for example, by the ancient Egyptians and in more recent times, American Indians. The reasons for using drugs and alcohol are as varied as the individuals who use them, and range from celebratory to attempting to gain insight into the future. The latter is especially true in connection with hallucinogens. For the purpose of this section, both drug and alcohol abuse will be regarded as the problem of substance abuse.

Some may argue that because substance abuse has been present ever since early civilisations it is not a specialist area nor even a psychiatric area, but rather a social problem. Drug advice centres or drug clinics can be seen as a necessity and a separate institute from the NHS. However it could also be argued that because substance abuse has been present for so long, the emergence of drug and alcohol abuse clinics is no more than a political expediency. However, I am sure that the professionals who come into contact with substance abusers would all agree that much pain and suffering is caused both physically and emotionally by this problem.

Many non-professionals see alcoholism as a biological addiction or the result of a destructive (marital) relationship. In terms of the model of this book, it would be fruitless to explore the cause and effect theories of substance abuse. The therapist should rather look at the interactions or communications which allow the abuse to continue. David Berenson (1976) states that if the therapist believes: 'any cause and effect explanation for alcoholism, she is ... incapable of effectively treating alcohol problems.' He also states that the therapist: 'must be willing to allow clients to accept cause and effect thinking such as the disease model of alcoholism if that will assist them in helping to resolve their drinking problem. The therapist therefore must not commit herself to any causative notion of alcoholism but act as if she had one.'

If one looks at the context of substance abuse in the concept of re-framing (see 'for example ... too much' on p. 107), it becomes apparent that in general terms there is nothing wrong with the drugs or alcohol but rather the method and extent to which they are used. If, for example, the heroin addict has sufficient money to finance his addiction, is able to provide sterile syringes and needles for his fix and is able to control the environment under which he gives way to his addiction, then to all intents and purposes there is no problem. Problems arise when the abuser commits criminal acts in order to finance his habit, or develops physical illnesses as a result of unhygienic intravenous administration or commits some form of public disorder or criminal offence while under the influence of the substance. The logic of the argument is that, in general terms, society does not see a problem with the actual substance but rather regarding the consequences or possible consequences of taking the substance to excess. If this attitude is adopted by the therapist when initiating treatment then her options of how to deal with the abuser are greatly increased, as are the possibilities of achieving therapeutic goals.

It seems pointless for the therapist to exhort, or make contractual arrangements with the abuser to exhibit willpower, since if he were able to do this it could be argued that he would not be in the situation of abusing. However if the therapist obtains detailed information regarding the behaviours and interactions surrounding the abuse, then by intervening in these patterns she can make it easier for the abuser to cease the habit.

If the client's presentation warrants immediate physical attention then the GP or local accident and emergency department should be involved. Such occasions include: alcoholic poisoning; acute withdrawal symptoms such as acute tremors, lack of concentration, restlessness and hallucinations; epileptic seizures; delerium tremens; tachycardia; heart failure and hyperventilation.

In addition to techniques described in previous chapters in relation to substance abusers, the technique of 'dangers of improvement' can be used. This involves relating to the client the greater stress which may result if he is able to control the abuse. For example:

THERAPIST: Would I be right in assuming from what you have previously said that you drink in order to escape the pressures of your job?

CLIENT: That's part of it. There's more to it than that. When I get home, because I've been drinking, my wife doesn't understand and arguments start at home.

THERAPIST: Well, it seems to me that although you seem what we call motivated, there may be greater problems for you to face if you were to cease drinking. For example, what kind of problems do you think would arise if you went home to your wife and had not been drinking? My guess is that she would be suspicious. What do you think?

CLIENT: Well, I really do want to stop drinking to the levels I have been because otherwise I am going to lose my job. But, I reckon what you say is right because I sometimes get the impression that my wife uses my drinking just to have a go at me.

By pointing out the dangers of improvement in this particular case the client is now in a position to accept the lesser goal, in his view, of controlled drinking rather than total abstinence.

This is a useful technique when the abuser states that his goal of therapy is complete cessation of the abuse and a re-achievement of normal living. It would be unwise for the therapist to accept this as a goal. The client could then insist that because the therapist has accepted his goal, she should remain in therapy with him until he has achieved his normal level of functioning. This is obviously unrealistic. By virtue of psychosocial transition, the client cannot achieve his previous levels. He must either surpass them or never achieve them. If the client even manages a small step forward, this is bound to be more encouraging than a continual struggle to reach a goal which was too high.

A technique which could also be used is acceleration of symptoms. But before initiating this technique, the therapist must be well aware of the circumstances surrounding the abuse and the client's beliefs, values and attitudes. For example:

THERAPIST: It seems to me that drinking to excess is a very painful process for you and accelerates the deterioration in your relationship with your wife. Am I correct?

CLIENT: Yes, that's right. The more the deterioration occurs, the more I drink.

THERAPIST: Would I also be correct in guessing that if you stopped drinking, the relationship between your wife and yourself might be resolved, although perhaps in a negative sense, in divorce?

CLIENT: Yes. There is no way now that I can go on with my wife even if I was sober.

THERAPIST: It seems to me that you are punishing yourself in a very painful way for finding yourself going down a one-way street and then trying to reverse back out of it. Perhaps the best thing for you to do would be to accelerate down the one-way street, come off the one-way system and then try to find your way back to wherever it was you were going. By this I mean that if your drinking is a method of accelerating a fruitless situation to its normal conclusion, then perhaps if you actually began to drink more, or seemed to be doing so, the situation would reach its conclusion sooner. Obviously there is extreme danger attached to this as, like the guy going down the one-way street, if you accelerate, you might hit some cars in front. But that is possibly no worse than what is happening just now because you may hit some cars as you reverse back down the one-way street. However in order to minimise the risks involved, I would be quite happy to see you daily to monitor the situation. I really hate to see people suffering as a result of circumstances and situations and it would seem only logical to accelerate this situation to its conclusion to end the pain and suffering. What do you think?

The client has been offered a logical conclusion to his conflict but in such a way as to achieve the goal he was presumably trying to avoid (divorce), and at the same time entailing possibly much more suffering. If the therapist has judged the client's beliefs and attitudes correctly, the client's only practical solution is to cut down or cease drinking and re-negotiate with his wife.

With drug abuse, especially in situations of prescribed medication abuse, contractual agreements are therapeutic. For example:

THERAPIST: Am I right in thinking that at present you take six times 5 mg per day? Would you like to come down to four times 5 mg per day?

CLIENT: Well, I'd like to get off Valium completely, but to begin with, that would be fine.

THERAPIST: OK. What I suggest is that you take six Valium one day, five the next, six the next, five the next and so on. I will call back in 2 weeks and we will then reduce it to five one day, four the next, five the next, four the next and so on. How would you feel about that?

CLIENT: What happens if I really need one in an emergency?

THERAPIST: What I would suggest in this situation is that when you are taking six and five, you keep one back for dire emergencies. That way you will always have one in stock.

CLIENT: Well, in that case I suppose it would be OK to try.

THERAPIST: If my arithmetic serves me right, for the first fortnight of one day on six tablets and one day on five tablets, you will need a total of 77 tablets. How many do you have at the moment?

CLIENT: I have a bottle of 100.

THERAPIST: OK. I do trust you and I'm sure you will keep to it, but just to remove temptation, I will take the excess 23 tablets and hold them for you. They can be added to your next batch.

Agreement must obviously be sought from the GP in any situation where the therapist is decreasing medication. There should also be close liaison with the GP to exclude manipulation by the client. One method of achieving this is to have three copies of a written contract: one copy is given to the client, one to the GP and the other is kept on file.

Other contractual methods would be to ascertain the time and circumstances under which the 'hard drug' abuser has his fixes. If for example they are early morning and early evening, the therapist could make a contract changing these times to late morning and late afternoon, or the dose could be changed to half-doses four times a day. It is common for the abuser to inject while on his own or at least to the exclusion of his family. It could be agreed that his family should monitor when he injects and how much. This is based on the theory that the continuance of abuse is only possible if patterns of abuse are followed. Therefore, by shifting the context or pattern of abuse, the therapist makes it more difficult or even impossible for the abuser to continue.

Obviously in the community it is more difficult to enforce or check on the circumstances of contracts. Even when clients are receiving drug substitutes, such as methadone, it is not unknown for them to sell this in order to obtain the real thing.

Although the use of urinalysis is an accurate guide to the client's intake of drugs, by implication it identifies a level of mistrust. This can be compared to the family of an alcohol abuser who believe they are being very therapeutic and constructive by locking all alcohol away so that the client does not have access or know where the key is kept. While this situation remains, there is a permanent air of mistrust. In many such cases the client is more likely to continue abusing.

Another technique which could be used for this client could be that of imminent failure. For example:

THERAPIST: It seems to me that you are well motivated and are prepared to undergo quite a bit of pain both emotionally and maybe physically to come off this stuff and I really don't know whether you realise exactly what you might be agreeing to.

CLIENT: I want to come off this stuff and I want to start now. I don't mind how much pain it takes.

THERAPIST: I appreciate your determination and have nothing but admiration for it. However, in my job I do see quite a lot of people who try to come off but I honestly do not know if you are going to be up to it or not, because determination is not enough.

Again the client has been given a relatively realistic view of what the imminent future holds as well as an implicit challenge to prove that he has the determination to come off the substance.

There are situations where families may be at risk from homicidal violence as a result of a family member abusing drugs or alcohol. In these cases, where necessary, it is appropriate for the client to be hospitalised for a short time. However it should be emphasised that hospitalisation in itself is no solution to the problem; the circumstances and interactions creating the desire or need for abuse must be dealt with. These can in fact be treated in the domestic situation while the client is being hospitalised and undergoing a withdrawal or detoxification programme.

It may be that the community psychiatric nurse or therapist is uneasy about taking on referrals of substance abusers and specialised clinics may be available in the locality. In these circumstances it would probably be advisable for the particular professional to refer the client to the specialist area. However if the professional is aware of the therapeutic programmes em-

ployed by the clinic, there is no reason why the initial ground-
work of therapy should not commence immediately. There is no
doubt that substance abuse is seen as a difficult area and the
therapist should always remember to work within her own limitations. A co-therapist or co-therapy team in this situation would
be of great advantage.

Children and Adolescents

Again, there are specialist centres and clinics for children and
adolescents and also community psychiatric nurses who special-
ise in this field. If the therapist feels uneasy about accepting
referrals of children and adolescents, it is recommended that she
should pass the referrals on appropriately. However the therapist
could do a lot of work before passing them on.

Many of the problems related to children and adolescents are
problems which the parents have difficulty in handling or coming
to terms with. For example, rebellion against authority, school
non-attendance, hyperactivity, depression or anxiety. It can be
seen from the life cycle events (Fig. 1.2; p. 6) that the majority of
transitions occur in childhood and the space between transitions
is relatively short compared with those in adulthood.

Children display a natural inquisitiveness and a need to learn
which make a huge demand on parents. From the parental point
of view, there is also perhaps a conflict of experience. This is
particularly highlighted in stepfamilies where there are two sets
of established patterns of managing children. No doubt the
therapist often hears the following statements from parents: 'My
parents brought me up very strictly and it didn't do me any harm,
so I'm going to do the same for my children. It's only right.' or
'My parents brought me up so strictly and rigidly that I fully
intend bringing my children up in the opposite way.' Both responses are equally correct. However, by definition of extreme-
ness, they do lay themselves open to criticism. For example, the
strict parent could be criticised for not learning the negative
aspects of too strict an upbringing. The parent in the second
example could be criticised for going to an equally negative
opposite extreme. Most parents will testify that there is nothing
easy about bringing up children, whether the children are seen to
behave 'normally' or 'abnormally'.

In the context of this therapy model, the difference lies in the parental response to the child's behaviour or demands. Again, most parents would testify that all children are demanding. However, as stated, the difference is not in how much or how often the child demands, but how the parent handles these demands. The intention of therapy should be to allow the parents to practise and experiment with different responses to the demands. Then the parents can choose the one that is most satisfactory in terms of the child's response and also the one which creates less demands for parents. It should be remembered that all children are born demanding, either for food or attention. Some children are less demanding than others and some have their demands met satisfactorily and some unsatisfactorily. As a result, therapy can often be more effective if directed at the parents, rather than at the individual child.

Hyperactivity or hyperkinesis is an area which is being paid increasingly more attention and which causes extreme distress to parents. Conners and Wells (1986) indicate that there are three possible types of therapy for these children:

1 Stimulant therapy.
2 Behavioural therapy, including social skills.
3 Multi-model therapies.

Their conclusions indicate that in the less disruptive child, stimulant therapy or behavioural therapy might be adequate but the multi-model method: 'may be necessary for highly disruptive hyperactive children who display the full range of symptomatology.' The multi-model method is a combination of stimulant therapy and behavioural therapy plus psychotherapy. However the authors do state that the relationship between parent and child is important and influential in the process of hyperkinesis.

From experience, the main component of difficulty for parents is a reluctance to follow the tasks set them. This can be because the parents feel that if the child displays such extreme behaviours, they as parents are not meeting the child's emotional or physical needs. The parents consequently feel guilty. If the tasks set emphasise the fact that the parents should become strict in the face of the demands put on them by the child, this could increase their level of existing guilt.

As stated earlier (p. 63), parents will present with one of two statements: 'This child is rebellious against my authority' or 'We are somehow not meeting the emotional demands of this child.' These statements are made irrespective of the degree or intensity of disruption which the child may be creating. It is therefore important for the therapist to identify clearly the stance of the parents in relation to the problem, that is, authoritarian or inadequate. The response should then be geared accordingly, even if the parental descriptions of the disruptive behaviours are identical.

There are many basic statements the therapist can use to enhance the position. For example:

THERAPIST: What do you think will happen if you continually give into your child's demands and he grows up seeking immediate gratification of his demands?

or:

THERAPIST: Quite often the best thing to do in order to be kind is to be cruel. Cruelty can be seen as subjective or objective. As parents, if you comply with the tasks I set, you will no doubt see yourselves as being cruel in the short term, whereas in the long term, you could objectively be seen as being kind. You are preparing your child for society and preparing his behaviour in such a way that society will not victimise him because of his behaviour.

Quite often a child's disruptive behaviour can be the result of parental disagreement on the upbringing of the child. They may disagree on levels of discipline, which demands should be met and which should not, or one parent stating one conclusion and the other parent another. If the child is told 'no' by one parent, it is quite common for him to go to the other parent and ask exactly the same question. If the parents do not communicate adequately, it is easy to see how the child can manipulate the indecision of both parents and create marital disharmony. It is therefore imperative for parents to employ a common strategy when dealing with their children, especially concerning discipline. This may be sufficient to minimise disruptive behaviour or at least to stop it from developing into a behavioural pattern which may continue or re-surface in adolescence.

Adolescence is a slightly different problem as the child is on the

verge of adulthood. He has a greater awareness of his environment and if he sees certain negative behaviours as being the result
of manipulation, then the opportunity for such manipulation
becomes greater. It is also much more difficult at this stage for
parents to exert any form of authority as there is the distinct
possibility of physical retaliation. Sally Brompton (1987) cites
many instances of adolescent violence: one case was a 23-year-
old man who stated that: 'his childhood aggression began when
he was six and he blames it on a troubled family background.
After his parents had divorced he came home from school one
day at the age of five to discover the body of his mother who had
gassed herself.' It appears this man became part of a reconstituted family (a stepfamily) and he: 'had to compete with four
other children for attention.' 'I was always on the edge of it. I was
terribly lonely and I felt left out.'

Reconstituted families or stepfamilies can be a major influence
in adolescent disruptive behaviour. In terms of family systems,
beliefs and attitudes, both sets of families have had a developed
system of dealing with problems and situations which need
adaptability. When these two families come together, there is a
need to re-negotiate and adapt both sets of attitudes. When this
happens, adolescents who have already been exposed to one
system find it more difficult to re-adapt from the old system. It is
very important for the therapist to be extremely empathic in this
situation.

In another example, Sally Brompton cites the case of a mother
who, when seeking support and help from the police, was told:
'You could always prosecute your son.' The mother's response
was appropriate and demanded an empathic response as she
stated: 'He is my son—my only son—and as a mother, you are
always hoping tomorrow's going to be different. Besides I'd be
very scared if he thought I was grassing on him.' This situation
demands a highly sensitive approach.

It should always be remembered, as previously stated, that as
children grow up they seek limits and boundaries for their own
behaviour. Adolescents are bound to hit brick walls in terms of
parental attitudes and disciplines. This process is commonly
termed the 'terrible teens'

One approach which seems to have results is parental fallibil-
ity. This obviously depends on the circumstances surrounding
the disruptive or aggressive behaviour. For example, there is the

case when an adolescent rebels against parental authority when asked to be home by a certain time. The advice given to the parents by the therapist would be: 'It would seem that when your child is out at night, you obviously and quite naturally worry and sit up biting your fingernails waiting for him to sneak in the door. When he does come through the door, I would imagine, from what you describe, that the ensuing process is both unrewarding and very confrontational. I would therefore suggest that you ask your child to be home by the usual time and if he is late, that you turn out the lights and lock the door and go to bed. I know as parents it would be unwise and totally impossible to ask you to go to sleep because of your parental worry. However, when your son comes home and tries the door and finds it locked, he is going to be puzzled. I would suggest that you wait for two or three minutes and then get up, put your light on, slowly walk downstairs and then unlock the door. As soon as you unlock the door you should apologise profusely to your son stating that you completely forgot he was out as it was so late and that you do not know how you could have forgotten to leave the door unlocked.'

In terms of interaction, if the parents employ this strategy, rather than confronting their son, they are actually apologising to him for their forgetfulness. It is much easier to become aggressive with somebody who is deliberately being aggressive towards you than somebody who is forgetful and perhaps genuinely did not realise the situation. Thus the confrontational aggressive aspect of the situation is diffused, with the parental option of continually re-employing it. This strategy can be re-enforced by various behaviours throughout the day towards the disruptive adolescent. Either of the parents could say for example: 'I am sorry I didn't get your tea. I forgot you were coming home. I thought you were going to your friend's house', or when turning the television up, stating: 'I'm sorry. I forgot you were upstairs trying to study.' Very soon the adolescent will realise that in order to enjoy the disruption caused, he must limit the extent of the disruption himself.

The technique of normalisation can also be used in this context. Frequently the behaviour complained of is in fact normal teenage behaviour, albeit very disruptive to the parents. By using the normalising technique, the therapist could ask each of the parents what they did as teenagers and whether or not they got into trouble with their own parents. This helps the parents put into perspective their parents' behaviour towards them and their own behaviour towards their child.

If an adolescent is exhibiting signs of depression, a very close watch should be kept on the level of depression. Factors such as: 'family disruption and rejection by parents ... a break in an important relationship, disciplinary crisis, isolation, lack of support and hopelessness' (Hawton, 1986) are regarded as frequent precipitants to adolescent suicide. It cannot be stressed enough that this area and those outlined previously cause much distress and anguish, not only to the client but also to the family members. It seems that the client is caught up in a cycle of behaviour which he cannot control. The parents are at a loss to know what to do for the best. It is therefore essential to promote an empathic, caring and sensitive approach.

Psychotic Clients

Family therapists and community agencies tend to be reluctant to deal with families in a family therapy setting if a member of that family is suffering from a psychotic illness. From experience it seems that this reluctance is restricted to what is termed 'schizophrenic families', rather than other psychotic illnesses such as manic–depressive psychosis or psychotic depression. Therefore for the purpose of this section, psychosis will be exemplified by the use of the word 'schizophrenia' but can in fact be deemed to cover all psychoses, other than organic.

Perhaps the reluctance to deal with schizophrenic families in family therapy is a result of the lack of knowledge about the causation of schizophrenia, the obvious unpredictability of behaviour and the incongruity of affect and lack of communicational skills sometimes shown by the schizophrenic.

Seeman *et al.* (1982) state that: 'A few theories are generally accepted: for example, a predisposition or vulnerability to schizophrenia may be passed from one generation to another. Since the symptoms usually first appear in the second or even third decade and not at birth, an age-specific hormonal or developmental trigger is required for schizophrenia to occur.' However, Argyle (1967) states: 'The disturbance of social behaviour is only one of the symptoms, but it is one of the most characteristic ones and it is a principal reason for their inability to deal with everyday life. They simply cannot communicate properly, or take part in ordinary social encounters.' Argyle then goes on to indicate three main theories or features. These have been interpreted as follows:

1 'Disturbed communication', where there is paradoxical communication or what is commonly known as 'the double bind'.
2 'There is a lack of concepts for persons': the schizophrenic has a deficiency 'of not being able to conceptualise persons or emotions'.
3 'A withdrawal from stressful social relationships' (Argyle, 1967).

In contrast, Paul Watzlawick (1977) states: 'Almost invariably there is a myth in these (schizophrenic) families that they have no problems and none of their members is unhappy about anything, except that they have a mental patient in their midst. But even a brief interview with them reveals glaring inconsistencies and reality distortions within the family as a whole.' He goes on to state: 'The schizophrenic patient, who is usually the most perceptive member of the family, lives in a world which is constantly defined for him as normal. It would be an almost superhuman task to resist this pressure to become a dissenter and expose the family myth. In all likelihood such an action would simply be considered further evidence of madness.' Watzlawick further says: 'He (the client) is faced with the dilemma of either risking rejection or sacrificing the evidence of his senses—and he is much more likely ... to choose the second alternative and remain a "patient".'

Philip Barker (1986) states: 'The evidence for biological component seems ... to be overwhelming and the efficacy of drug therapy is apparently greater than that of conventional family therapy. It is also clear that genetic factors are involved.'

Some of the above indicates what Philip Barker reiterates in his book *Basic Family Therapy* (1986): 'Children of schizophrenics placed early for adoption in non-schizophrenic families still develop schizophrenia at rates higher than the population rates, sometimes as high as those reared by their schizophrenic parents; adoptive relatives of schizophrenics do not have elevated rates of schizophrenia but the biological relatives of the adoptees do have higher rates.'

Throughout most books on the subject of schizophrenia two main concepts are constantly referred to:

1 The double bind theory.
2 Expressed emotion.

It should be clarified at this point that none of these authors claims that any one factor causes schizophrenia but rather that each factor contributes greatly to the predisposition of schizophrenia

Before moving on to the practical implications of therapy when there are psychotic family members present, it would be beneficial to look at the concepts of the double bind theory and expressed emotion, which appear to have greatly influenced modern thinking on schizophrenia.

The first written conceptualisation of the double bind appeared in a paper written by Gregory Bateson, Don Jackson, Jay Haley and John Weakland called *Toward a Theory of Schizophrenia* (1968). This paper was the result of a research project which had been carried out between 1952 and 1954. The authors defined the double bind not as any specific trauma but rather a sequential pattern. They also indicated that these sequences must have certain characteristics and: 'from them (the sequences) the patient will acquire the mental habits which are exemplified in schizophrenic communication. That is to say, he must live in a universe where the sequence of events are such that his unconventional communication habits will be in some sense appropriate.' The authors then described the six steps forming the process of the double bind, as follows:

1 'Two or more persons.' Because interaction and communication can only be defined in terms of more than one person, two or more persons are therefore required for this process to take place. The authors clearly indicated that this process does not depend on the mother alone but can be any combination of mother, father, siblings.
2 'Repeated experience.' Here it is indicated that in order for the double bind to become effective, there must be a recurrent theme in the experience of what is termed 'the victim'. Repeated experiences of double bind become a habitual expectation.

3 'A primary negative injunction.' This injunction can be such statements as: 'Do not do this or I will punish you' or 'If you do not do this I will punish you'. This is the process of learning based on avoidance of punishment rather than on reward-seeking. Punishment can be defined as either the withdrawal of love, or the expression of hate or anger. Another form of punishment for the child may be the implied expression of parental helplessness.

4 'A secondary injunction conflicting with the first at a more abstract level and like the first, enforced by punishment or signals which threaten survival.' The authors state that the secondary injunction tends to be more on a non-verbal level, using posture, gesture, tone of voice and the implications concealed in verbal comment. The secondary injunction may impinge on the primary injunction and as a result, may include a varied form of verbalisation. For example: 'Do not see this as punishment' or 'Don't see me as the punishing person.' The variety of this injunction becomes endless when more than one person is involved in inflicting the injunctions. For example, one person may undermine or negate what the first person said at an abstract level.

5 'A tertiary negative injunction prohibiting the victim from escaping from the field.' Here the authors state that this injunction may not necessarily be a separate item, since re-enforcement of steps 3 and 4 may prove sufficient because, if these double binds are imposed at an early age, the young child is physically less able to escape. However methods are used which are not necessarily negative in this area, for example, promises of love etc.

6 'The complete set of ingredients is no longer necessary when the victim has learned to perceive his universe in double bind patterns.' That is, any part of the double bind sequence may then be sufficient to bring on rage or panic.

The authors argue that this pattern of conflicting injunction may be taken over by hallucinatory voices. They also point out that there are predisposing factors which may induce breakdown in the double bind situation. That is, the double bind *on its own* may or may not produce breakdown. Most families employ the double bind at some point, especially with children. The predisposing factors are:

1 'When the individual is involved in an intense relationship.'
2 'The individual is caught in a situation in which the other person in the relationship is expressing two orders of message and one of these denies the other.'
3 'The individual is unable to comment on the messages being expressed to correct his discrimination of what order of message to respond to, that is, he cannot make a metacommunicative statement' (Bateson *et al.*, 1968).

A metacommunicative statement in this context is a statement relating to the rules and guidelines on which communication is transmitted and received.

As an example of this bizarre method of communication and the practical consequences it may have for the client, for other family members and possibly also for the therapist, here is an incident taken from personal experience:

THERAPIST: Could you tell James (not visibly present) that I'm here to see him?

MOTHER: He's upstairs in bed. He's been up there all day and I don't think he'll come down.

THERAPIST: Could you tell him I'm here to see him?

MOTHER: He won't come down, you know. He stays in bed most of the day.
(Mother then turns radio on and turns the volume up loudly.)

THERAPIST: I'm sorry—could you please tell James that I am here to see him?

MOTHER: I just have.

THERAPIST: Could you go up to his bedroom and tell him that I'm here to see him?

MOTHER: Very well, but it won't do any good.
(Mother then turns the record player on at loud volume.)

THERAPIST: (Shouting above the noise of radio and record player) Could you please go up to James' bedroom and tell him that I am here to see him?

MOTHER: You mean actually go up the stairs and knock on his bedroom door? He's still asleep you know.

THERAPIST: Yes. That is what I would like you to do.

MOTHER: (Goes upstairs and taps lightly on James's bedroom door, shouting down the stairs)

He won't get up.

THERAPIST: Could you please knock a little louder to let him know you are there and that I wish to see him?

MOTHER: (Knocks loudly on James's door. Suddenly from James's bedroom comes the noise of his radio on full blast. Mother comes back downstairs and says)

You see what I have to put up with. I have to put up with this crazy behaviour non-stop.

This situation took place at 3 o'clock one afternoon. Once the radio and record player had been turned off, the mother was asked why she had turned them on in the first place rather than follow the request to go upstairs and rouse her son. She responded by saying that this was her normal way of indicating to her son that it was time he got out of bed, despite defining her son's behaviour as 'crazy', which in communicational context was appropriate. The therapist then went up to James's bedroom and asked if he would get dressed and come downstairs, to which he replied that he would have come down earlier if he had known the therapist was there.

This example clearly indicates the unconventional methods of communication which exist in such families. When presented to an outsider they certainly seem bizarre and perhaps even psychotic, although in their contexts, they are in fact relatively normal.

The onset of schizophrenia is commonly perceived as stress-induced. It can be suggested that when stress becomes too great, the client will move towards an existence which avoids the reality of pressures or towards a fantasy existence. However if the client does this, he must obviously make sure that he cannot be recalled from his fantasy. As such, delusions are then expressed with the back-up of hallucinations to prove their existence. As delusions are not usually within the therapist's concept of reality, it becomes very difficult to communicate with the client. To achieve this level, the client must adopt a delusion powerful enough to deny the logical reasoning of the therapist, hence such statements as: 'I am God' or 'I am Jesus' or 'There is no existence outside this room' etc.

RMN training teaches that when faced with delusions, the nurse should not confront or collude with such statements; however, no other alternative is proposed. The nurse is therefore powerless. There is no doubt that both collusion and confrontation with psychotic clients are detrimental and dangerous, but training does not normally give the option of confronting the delusion from within the delusion. To do this, the therapist should remember that, because of habitual experience, the client actually believes what he is saying. The following is an example of a personal experience of confrontation from within a delusion.

A client presented to the local accident and emergency department in a distressed state, stating that he was God. The psychiatric emergency service was contacted. As a result of confrontation and collusion by the staff in the accident and emergency department, the client became more and more agitated and aggressive. When the therapist arrived, the client was pacing quickly up and down the corridor exclaiming in a loud voice that he was God and had come to avenge the sins committed by society. The conversation went as follows, during which time the therapist was actually pacing up and down the corridor with the client:

THERAPIST: I believe you believe that you are God.

CLIENT: Yes, of course I am God. I know everything and I have come to punish society for all the wrongs and sins that they have committed.

THERAPIST: Don't you recognise me?

CLIENT: Why should I recognise you?

THERAPIST: I believe that I am Jesus Christ, therefore I am your son.

CLIENT: (Now standing still)
You're not my son. I don't recognise you.

THERAPIST: Am I right that you believe you're God and I believe I'm Jesus?

CLIENT: Well, I know that I am God, but I don't recognise you.

THERAPIST: I believe I am Jesus, therefore I am your son and as you know the Holy Ghost moves in mysterious ways. It is my belief that as Jesus Christ I can adopt any physical form to do my job.

CLIENT: You must be bloody mad. Do you really believe you are Jesus Christ?

THERAPIST: I believe I am if you believe you are God.

CLIENT: That's bloody nonsense.
THERAPIST: If that's the case, why don't we sit down quietly and talk about whatever your problem is?
CLIENT: Well, the real problem is that I am worried sick about my parents.

From that moment, as a result of being confronted within his delusional system as opposed to outside it, the client ceased his delusional patterns of thinking and verbalising. This process is based on the belief that such clients attempt to escape the pressures of reality by moving into the delusions of fantasy. However, when faced with the possibility of responsibilities within that fantasy, the only way to opt out is to go back to what is termed 'reality'. In this particular case, the client's delusions and hallucinations ceased from that moment, although approximately 7 to 10 days later he commenced chemotherapy. However in the intervening space he was free from the delusions and accompanying agitation. It transpired that the client had received a communication from his mother informing him that since he had left home, his father had started drinking heavily and on one occasion had returned home drunk and physically attacked the mother. In this situation it can be seen that a 'schizophrenic episode' was a way of avoiding pressure. He was not colluding with either of his parents by returning home or siding with one or the other. Instead, he became 'ill', which might necessitate his return home, albeit superficially against his will, and as a result he could not be seen as a failure in his parents' eyes.

In terms of life cycle events, this process is most liable to occur when a child leaves home and begins to become independent, that is, in the mid-20s. As stated previously, if the son returned home, the parents would no longer need to renegotiate their own relationship as individuals because they would have to revert to the mother or father role and look after the 'ill' son.

Expressed emotion (EE) or emotional expressiveness and the measurement of it—high or low—in families was first proposed in 1972 by Brown *et al*. Other studies carried out throughout the world tended to confirm the findings of Brown's study, that where there is a high emotional expressiveness in families, there is an increased probability of schizophrenic relapse. In an earlier study in 1962 Brown found that: 'Drugs did not seem to have a protective effect in the low emotional expressive group, but did in the high emotional expressive group.' Also: 'Low face to face contact had no effect in the low EE group, but was significantly related to lower relapse rates in the high EE group.'

As reported in Barker's interpretation of Brown's studies, emotional expressiveness was measured: 'using scales developed over a period of years' (Barker, 1986). These scales: 'involve a recognition of particular comments (critical and positive) and consist of a count of all such comments occurring at any one point in the interview.' Also: 'emotional over-involvement, hostility and warmth—involve the recognition of particular kinds of comments: the interviewer then makes a judgement of the degree to which the emotion concerned was shown.' This concept also obviously involves the model of interactional and communicational theories.

Atkinson (1986) indicates the cultural factors which may be influential in expressed emotion and states: 'In London most families fall into the low EE group, whereas in California only one-third of the families were rated as being low on expressed emotion. Hostility was also rated as being more common in California than London.'

There is therefore no known causation of schizophrenia, although there are various methods or models which indicate an understanding of the process of schizophrenia. It is up to the therapist to decide which process would be most therapeutic in terms of family therapy.

One point which coincides with the overall process of schizophrenia is that of the patient's distractability. By using this distractability the therapist can calm down a potentially violent client or an aggressive situation.

One other method of intervention the therapist could use, but in general terms should be avoided, is 'direct communicational confrontation'. This technique depends on the presentation, confidence and experience of the therapist and, more importantly, on the client's physical and mental presentation. If the therapist feels comfortable using this technique, it can prove beneficial and therapeutic. An example of this technique is as follows:

THERAPIST: It seems to me that there is a communicational problem within this family and for whatever reason John (the identified client) tends to communicate in such a way that nobody can understand him.

FATHER: That's quite correct. We often find that if we ask him to do things, he then begins to speak in gobbledegook.

THERAPIST TO JOHN: It seems to me that you are under a lot of pressure just now. What do you think about what has already been said?

JOHN: If the sun reversed its oscillation round Mars, then the trees would not be polluted by acid rain nor would we have trouble with all these Communist spies.

THERAPIST: John, if you don't stop speaking rubbish then I see no point in carrying on or trying to help you understand what is going on. I am therefore asking you to reply to my questions in a way that you know I will understand.

JOHN: 'Well, OK.'

Confrontational communicational methods may aggravate agitation, hostility or even aggression and the therapist should be very confident that she can carry this procedure off.

Regarding the setting in which to interview such clients or families, it is suggested that in view of the multiple levels of communication which exist within such families and the distractability that pervades such systems, it is much easier if the therapist has co-therapists either behind a screen or in the same room. It can be very difficult for a single community worker to assimilate all verbal and non-verbal levels of communication, although it is possible for her to be aware of the individual who appears to be issuing conflicting messages (double bind) in therapy. She can then request clearer information regarding his responses and, by using such techniques, can indicate to the client methods of pinning down this abstract communication so that it cannot become a double bind.

It is known that tranquillising drugs control the symptoms of schizophrenia. Although it appears incongruous to believe in the concepts of family therapy and at the same time appear to re-enforce the concept of the medical model of medication, it can be seen that there is a place for both and, in this model of family therapy, they are not mutually exclusive. It is relatively simple to state to a client: 'The doctor believes this medication will help you. I would also like to help, but as I am not a doctor, my methods may be somewhat different.' The attraction of this model of family therapy is that it does allow the co-existence of all other models. There is therefore no conflict between the progressive community worker and the institutional worker. Both exist within their own rights and both have an important part to play.

As stated at the beginning of this section, although schizophrenia was the psychosis discussed, the concepts also apply to all other psychoses.

Ethnic Minorities

The adjective 'ethnic' indicates the values, attitudes and beliefs which make one culture different from another. Ethnic minorities can create tremendous problems for the therapist if she is unable or unwilling to accept these alternative values, attitudes and beliefs.

There are cultural differences within the British Isles which are historically inherent. The culture of Scottish people differs from that of the English, as does that of the Welsh and the Irish. One example of the most commonly visible evidence of cultural differences is associated with death. In certain parts of the north of Scotland, if a spouse dies, it is quite common for the surviving spouse to wear black (in itself a cultural value) for several years following the death. In Ireland it is a common cultural attitude to hold a wake following death. These cultural differences extend to the time allocated for grief. It can be argued that there have always been ethnic minorities and cultural differences within the historical indigenous population of the British Isles.

The term 'ethnic minorities' does perhaps have an associated negative imagery, possibly due to media coverage and presentation. Perhaps a better phrase would be 'differing cultures'. To a large degree, ethnic minorities or differing cultures depend on circumstances and on one's perception. For example, a Scottish Highlander living in his birthplace would not be referred to as an ethnic minority. However, that same person living in the heart of London could be regarded as such, as he would be of a different culture to the majority of people within that environment.

Civilisations throughout history have always been quick to project their own fears on to others of a different cultural persuasion and whether or not these fears are justified is irrelevant. Civilisations frequently blame their own short-comings on the minority which happens to be available at the time, for example, the Roman civilisation and the early Christians; the Germans during the Second World War and the Jews; the Ku-Klux-Klan in America and the southern Negroes. It is very easy to point the finger at others rather than look to oneself for blame and by rationalisation, this process absolves the person pointing the finger from any guilt.

In systemic terms, when two cultures come together (as in stepfamilies) there is usually a clash, especially when the cultures differ in major areas. This is usually followed by a generational compromise. As the two cultures exist together in close proximity there will be an overflow from one to the other, with the modifications and compromises taking place in both cultures, and a third new amalgamated culture emerges.

Communication is one of the biggest problems in varying cultures. Sugden *et al.* (1986) quote an example as follows: 'The potential exists in most British mental hospitals for the native patient to talk to an Irish nurse, who passes on the message to his Caribbean and Malaysian colleagues, who in turn will talk to the Indian doctor. The potential for the message to be misconstrued or misunderstood as it passes through the many cultural filters is great.' Yet again, there is a need for clear, specific data and information to be gleaned from the client and to be transmitted on to other professionals clearly and specifically. The scope of cultural and ethnic differences is limitless. As Burnham (1986) states: 'Ethnic groups have specific rituals'. He cites as examples the Jewish bar mitzvah which helps in the transition from adolescence to adulthood and the Irish wake which helps in the transition towards acceptance of death.

Another area of possible confusion or difficulty is individual family rules and myths. In some cultures it is an accepted family rule that the eldest male child will financially provide for the retired parents if necessary; that the eldest unmarried daughter will physically care for the ageing parents; that one member of the family (usually one of the senior members) will remain physically close to the parents' home to be available if needed. Therefore familial attitudes, beliefs and values within the overall umbrella of that culture assimilate idiosyncratic behaviours without actually appearing to be beyond the norm.

Field, writing in Sugden *et al.* (1986) makes the following pertinent point: 'West Indians are more likely to be diagnosed as schizophrenic; and people from Northern Ireland are more frequently admitted with alcoholism than a person from England or

Wales. Is this because people who migrate are more likely to be mentally ill? Or is it because immigrants are more likely to suffer social disadvantage and racism, and hence be socially and economically deprived, thus making them more prone to mental illness due to poor housing, lack of amenities and high unemployment?' He then goes on to ask: 'Could it be also that the person from another culture communicates illness in a different way and is therefore misunderstood by the native?'

There is no doubt that the various cultures perceive the same phenomenon differently. For example, the majority of Western civilisations sees death as a loss, whereas the older culture of the American Indians sees death as a freeing of the soul and therefore something to be celebrated. This does not mean that one is right and one is wrong; both are equally right and valid from the individual's culture perception. If problems arise as a result of perceptual conflict either in terms of the individual and his own culture, or the individual and another culture, then it is important to remember that the individual's perception is correct for him. There are therefore two forms of problems which will occur with ethnic minorities: problems occurring within the particular culture and problems occurring as a result of a clash between two differing cultures. Problems arising within a particular culture can be dealt with as previously outlined by the use of psychosocial transition and the associated varying skills and techniques.

However, if that culture differs from that of the therapist, she has a responsibility to identify the laws, rules, rituals and idiosyncrasies of that culture in order to be more therapeutically effective. It is therefore important for the therapist to judge the client's level and language accurately as well as using empathy within the cultural setting.

Due to the multiplicity of potential problems, it is perhaps easier to give examples of what not to do rather than what to do. For example, it would be unwise, perhaps potentially dangerous and certainly therapeutically disastrous for a non-Indian therapist to confront the parental authority of an Indian family. It may be constructive and part of boundary-searching in some cultures to probe and push parental authority without question. However, in some cultures, for example Indian and Chinese, one of the rules may be that parental authority is never questioned. By confronting the issue the therapist would therefore go totally against the grain of the cultural values and attitudes as well as, in all probability, the familial beliefs, irrespective of idiosyncratic behaviours within that particular family. It would be equally inappropriate for a non-West Indian therapist to use certain types of West Indian jargon. Although the therapist may believe this is a way of improving communication, it may be seen by the client as condescending, sarcastic and may invoke hostility.

The therapist's basic principle must therefore be respect for the client's culture, irrespective of whether or not she believes or agrees with the cultural attitudes. Identifying the cultural beliefs and how strongly they are held can be done relatively easily by the therapist. One solution would be for the therapist to read up on the cultural values and attitudes of whichever group she comes into contact with. Another possible method would be to use trial and error, although in therapeutic terms this is not advisable due to possible trauma to both client and therapist. A third and perhaps more simple method would be for the therapist to try and gain some insight into cultural values by going back through the life cycle events of the client and gaining information on his responses. For example:

THERAPIST: How long have you been depressed?

CLIENT: Ever since my father died 2 years ago.

THERAPIST: Could you tell me what the family did when your father died?

CLIENT: The entire family got together and money was raised by my uncles to help us out, but that doesn't seem to have been enough.

THERAPIST: Out of your family network, who would your mother be expected to go to if she wanted help?

CLIENT: She is supposed to go to the eldest uncle.

THERAPIST: Who would you be expected to go to if you wanted help or support.

CLIENT: I would be expected to go to my oldest brother.

THERAPIST: Have you tried any of these avenues so far?

CLIENT: Yes, I have, but I don't seem to be getting anywhere.

For the purpose of this example, the aspect of obtaining cultural information regarding values and attitudes has been highlighted rather than the aspect of clinical depression and its causation.

The above example indicates the methods used by that particular culture to cope, the avenues they are expected to explore for help and the hierarchical structure. It also shows the cultural attitudes towards the extended family which, in times of death, are brought into the nuclear family and can have a similar role to that of the nuclear family in providing financial support, physical support and so on. It also shows that within this particular culture, the male (usually the oldest) is seen as the provider and organiser. Therefore, from such a short example, cultural attitudes and values have been elicited and the therapist must remember that although these may not be her attitudes or values, she must take them into consideration and utilise them within the framework of cultural rules to make therapy successful.

Religious belief or lack of it is one of the greatest cultural differences both internal and external to Britain. It has been known for nurses to try to impose the comfort and security of their own religion on to clients of differing religions or even on to clients with no religious beliefs. Needless to say, this approach meets with negative responses. Religion is, in itself, a set of beliefs and even a philosophy for life and as each individual perceives life differently, his own perceptions should be respected.

In terms of intercultural relationships or marriages, the issue of negotiation and mediation, although not simple, is clearer. This can be helped by an understanding of the cultures involved, as well as specific information regarding the actual problem. For example:

THERAPIST TO HUSBAND: From what you are saying, and correct me if I'm wrong, I get the impression that you believe that your wife should be obedient in matters where you have to make the decision.

HUSBAND: That is correct, because where I come from, what the man says goes. I'm the one who is out working all day, so I should have a say in what goes on in my own house.

THERAPIST TO WIFE: Am I correct in thinking that you make all the domestic decisions such as what meals to cook and when the children should go to bed or who is responsible for what within the house?

WIFE: That's right. He sees it as my job to run the house but not to question any decision he makes regarding the family as a whole.

THERAPIST: It seems to me that the problem is not that anyone is falling down on his responsibilities but that both of you are taking your responsibilities maturely and seriously—but like everything else in life, there are areas of overlap. I may be wrong, but it seems that this overlap seems to occur, particularly in your situation, in terms of responsibility and authority within the house. As a result, neither of you are sure what the other is doing or where the responsibility of the other ends. Therefore to make sure that the domestic scene of family life runs as smoothly as possible, both of you are assuming that the other is not making a decision in that particular area. You therefore end up with two different decisions on the same issue, which will obviously cause arguments.

By positively re-framing this situation, the therapist has validated both points of view and in this case, both cultural attitudes. At the same time she has indicated that there is room for negotiation in a specific area without challenging any cultural values. The therapist could then go on to suggest that both partners get together to clarify the common ground. Having done this, it may then be possible, if considered appropriate by the client, to negotiate from the centre line outwards into other areas, which may produce overt cultural conflict. However, as soon as the therapist reaches an area of cultural conflict, if mediation is not fruitful, it may be best to positively re-frame the situation so that for the moment at least, the area is left under the question mark of future negotiation. By doing this the therapist has at least achieved a resolution to the initial problem and highlighted the need for mediation and negotiation within the cultures. The art of negotiation in many family problems is finding out what each is prepared to give to get what he wants.

Each culture has positive aspects, otherwise, by definition, it would not have been adopted as a culture or method of functioning. It is advantageous for the therapist to discover and highlight the positive aspects of any given culture, rather than dwell on the negative aspects when dealing with people from that culture. In all human behaviours, if the positive features are highlighted and encouraged, the negative aspects, by implication, seem less important. It also means that the therapist comes across in these situations with empathy, understanding and a caring attitude.

From experience, the greatest fault of community agencies towards ethnic minorities or, in the broader context, differing cultures, seems to be a lack of understanding and a rejection of that culture because it does not comply with the individual's perception of life in terms of values, attitudes and beliefs. As already indicated, each perception is neither right nor wrong but is valid and demands respect.

Summary

No summary is offered for this chapter as each section is in itself a summary.

Exercises

Sexual Problems

1 In any families you see with prepubertal children, do any fit in with predisposing factors or symptoms of abuse or incest?
2 Discuss with colleagues the best *team* approach to such suspected cases (that is, the best collection of individual approaches and co-therapy approaches).
3 When dealing with rape cases, assess your own level of balance between legal requirements and therapeutic strategy.
4 Make a point of asking the victim to write down her recollections and validate the perceptions and emotions given.
5 Ask the client to describe the interactional or communicational pattern which results in sexual dysfunction.
6 The next time the client uses a particular level of language (for example, prick instead of penis), respond in his or her language and monitor firstly, the speed at which therapy progresses and secondly, the level of uneasiness or otherwise shown.
7 Check that there is free passage of information between the partners relating to needs, wishes, desires and fulfilment.

Substance Abuse

8 When next dealing with substance abusers, use the re-frame of '... too much' and monitor both client and family response.
9 Identify what the client is trying to escape from and how others highlight and perhaps maybe even promote this behaviour by their interaction.

10 Having established a pattern of behaviour, change it in some way, either in the context of time, place, intensity or people.

Children and Adolescents

11 When dealing with rebellious or aggressive children, ask the parents if their parents ever felt in a similar way about them.
12 Sometimes just say to the child in a benevolent way: 'I know your game' and refuse to enlarge. Assess the child's and parents' responses.

Psychotic Clients

13 Itemise the more common delusions of your clients. Think of ways to confront this from within the delusion in such a way that there is implicit or explicit pressure of responsibility on the client.
14 Where there is evident communicational problems, challenge for a more practical definition of what is meant. Continue to do so until a clear, specific message is offered.
15 Try to identify the double bind in interactions and communications. (Non-verbal behaviour can constitute this, for example, offering love while obviously tense and unhappy.)

Ethnic Minorities

16 Identify your own cultural beliefs, values, attitudes or myths which would make you a minority in a different culture.
17 When interviewing a client from a minority, subtly direct the questioning towards how his family responded during the last major transition. Identify the differences and validate the client.
18 Show an interest in the client's culture at the expense of half an hour of therapy. Note the difference in flow and ease of therapy thereafter.

References

Abramowicz, M. (1983) Drugs that cause sexual dysfunction. *Medical Letter*; 25: 73–6.
Argyle, M. (1967). *The Psychology of Interpersonal Behaviour*. London, Penguin, pp. 171–4.

Atkinson, J. M. (1986). *Schizophrenia at Home: A Guide to Helping the Family*. London, Croom Helm.

Barker, P. (1986). *Basic Family Therapy*, 2nd edn. London, Collins.

Bateson, G., Jackson, D. D., Haley, J., Weakland, J. H. (1968). Toward a theory of schizophrenia. In: Jackson, D. D. (ed.) *Communication, Family and Marriage*. Palo Alto, Science and Behaviour Books, pp. 31–54.

Berenson, D. (1976). Alcohol and the Family System. In: Guerin, P. (ed.) *Family Therapy: Theory and Practice*. New York, Gardner Press.

Brompton, S. (1987). Parents who live in fear. *The Times*; 8 June p. 21.

Brown, G. W., Birley, J. L. T., Wing, J. K. (1972). Influence of family life on the course of schizophrenic disorder. *British Journal of Psychiatry*; 121: 241–58.

Burnham, J. B. (1986). *Family Therapy*. London, Tavistock Publications.

Conner, C. K., Wells, K. C. (1986). *Hyperkinetic Children: A Neuropsychosocial Approach*. London, Sage Publications, pp. 124–41.

Friesen, J. D. (1985). *Structural–Strategic Marriage and Family Therapy*. London, Gardner Press, pp. 87–9.

Hawton, K. (1986). *Suicide and Attempted Suicide Among Children and Adolescents*. London, Sage Publications, p. 139.

Kaplan, H. S. (1978). *The New Sex Therapy*. London, Penguin.

Masters, W. H., Johnson, V. E. (1966). *Human Sexual Response*. Boston, Little, Brown.

Minde, K., Minde, R. (1986). *Infant Psychiatry: An Introductory Textbook*.

Seeman, M. V., Littmann, S. K., Plummer, E., Thornton, J. F., Jeffries, J. J. (1982). *Living and Working with Schizophrenia*. Milton Keynes, Open University Press, pp. 6–12.

Sugden, J., Bessant, A., Eastland, M., Field, R. (1986). *A Handbook for Psychiatric Nurses*. London, Harper & Row.

Watzlawick, P. (1977). *How Real is Real?* New York, Vintage Books, pp. 88–9.

Further Reading

Bateson, G., Jackson, D. D., Haley, J., Weakland, J. H. (1962). A note on the double bind. *Communication, Family and Marriage*, vol. 1. Palo Alto, Science and Behaviour Books.

Bullard D., Knight, S. (1981). *Sexuality and Physical Disability: Personal Perspectives*. St Louis, C. V. Mosby.

Everstine, D. S., Bodin, A. M., Everstine, L. (1977). Emergency psychology *Family Process*; 16: 281–92.

McFarlane, K., Waterman, J. (1987). *Sexual Abuse of Young Children*. Guildford Press, New York.

O'Hanlon, W. H., Wilk, J. (1987). *Shifting Contexts: The Generation of Effective Therapy*. Guildford Press, New York.

Watzlawick, P. (1962). A review of the double bind theory. *Communication, Family and Marriage*, vol. 1. Palo Alto, Science and Behaviour Books.

8

Saying Goodbye or Hello Again

Discharge is a little recognised skill and tends to be left until the last minute! (MacPhail, 1986).

Discharge from treatment should be a well thought out, planned process and not a spontaneous reaction by the therapist. Discharging the client or family from therapy is part of the treatment process and should therefore be given an equal amount of forethought. The timing and presentation of the discharge process can greatly influence not only the therapeutic outcome, but also the possibility of a statement such as 'Hello again'.

Discharge or termination of therapy usually occurs as the result of one of two reasons: the client wishes therapy to finish or the therapist wishes therapy to finish. Obviously the reasons behind the decision, made either by client or therapist, vary depending on the circumstances.

If the client or family wishes to end treatment, this may arise in several different ways. For example, the family may just stop attending sessions in clinic-based practices or they may continually arrive late, usually with important members of the family missing. The family may become critical of the therapist's methods or perceptions. They may begin to lose interest, generally in the course of therapy and particularly in the achievement of tasks set. Perhaps the client or family consider they have reached a sufficient level which does not warrant further treatment. If any of the above 'symptoms' occur, the therapist has two choices: to venture the prospect of termination of treatment herself, or to wait for the family to indicate this move. With the second option, treatment will be unnecessarily extended, probably with little therapeutic value. If it becomes evident that the family no longer wishes to continue with therapy, the therapist should assess what progress has been achieved in therapy and whether or not this is sufficient to give the family the inclination to terminate. She should also assess at this point whether or not

157

termination of treatment would prove detrimental to the functioning of the family. This evaluation is more therapeutic if done by the therapist in agreement with and in the presence of the family concerned. After assessing the goals achieved and the current level of functioning, the therapist and family may agree that therapy should terminate. In this case, the therapist should check the circumstances of the family as a whole and individually to ascertain the existence of any situation which could threaten any progress made. If any situation becomes apparent, then the techniques of prediction of relapse or prescription of relapse can be employed. For example:

THERAPIST: James, it seems to me that we've reached the natural conclusion to our sessions. I get the impression that you are keen to finish coming here and if possible, you would like to get straight back to work.

CLIENT: Yes, that's right. I feel a lot better, a lot more confident in myself and I must admit I'm beginning to get bored at home and would like to get back to work as soon as possible.

THERAPIST: How do you think you will find things at work?

CLIENT: I know it's going to be tough to begin with, but once I get back into the swing of things, there is no reason why I can't do my job just as well as I did before.

THERAPIST: I'm really pleased about this, but I am a little surprised at this sudden burst of enthusiasm. I just hope it doesn't cloud your judgement. I'm sure it won't. Do you see any problems arising at home or at work, if you return to work?

CLIENT: I don't see why there should be any problems. I feel perfectly fit ... more like my old self.

THERAPIST: I certainly admire your enthusiasm and determination, but I think I would be a little happier in myself if I saw some healthy apprehension. I'm not trying to detract from the fact that you have obviously done well and that the family situation has improved, but I just get the feeling that things may not run as smoothly as you possibly think they might. I don't want to put a damper on your spirits, but could we possibly spend 5 minutes just looking at the possibilities?

CLIENT: OK, if you want to, but I'm sure things will be fine.

THERAPIST: Perhaps I won't put a damper on things. Maybe we

could just look at how much you've achieved in therapy. Do you remember the situation when you initially came here? Things were pretty bad then. I just wonder if you have any idea what brought that process about.

CLIENT: Well, I'm not sure about the process, but I certainly remember the situation when I first needed help.

THERAPIST: It seems to me that these kind of situations sneak up on us and before we know it, we're slap bang in the middle of them. With all the best intentions in the world, you may find that these situations sneak up on you again, not necessarily regarding your problem, but maybe a different problem.

CLIENT: I'm sure I can handle it next time.

THERAPIST: I'm sure you can, but it seems to me that when situations sneak up on us, we tend to lose sight of what we did to resolve previous problems, usually because of the habit of certain behaviours. It might be a good idea, whenever things get a bit tough again, for you to accelerate this process so that this, in turn, will accelerate the capabilities you now have to resolve problems. That way you will not forget how to handle difficulties successfully. I would suggest that if you don't have any problems in the first 3 months, you actually create a problem so that these coping mechanisms will be re-awakened. That way, they will not lie dormant and eventually be forgotten.

This conversation indicates that although the therapist validates and accepts the enthusiasm and perhaps over-optimism of the client in terms of discharge and 'Life will be fine from now on', the client is also requested to retain a healthy pessimism about how smoothly life actually runs. This process is partially normalising as well as indicating that there may be relapse in the future. By specifically requesting the client to relapse, if a relapse occurs, he will not be caught up in negative cycles of attempting to solve the problem because the therapist has already indicated that relapse is part of the prescription and is therefore under control. As well as redefining the relapse, this is also a training experience for the client. If a relapse does not occur and the client follows the therapist's instructions and promotes one, then again by definition, this must be under the client's control. However, if a relapse does not occur and the client does not prescribe his own relapse, again by implication, the client is managing to function adequately.

In a situation where the client insists on discharge from treatment against the better wishes or judgement of the therapist, the above technique can be employed, but slightly more forcefully. For example:

THERAPIST: I can understand your wish to finish treatment and can see the progress that you've made which seems to qualify your decision. However, it seems to me that you could be throwing away any progress you have achieved, on impulse. However, I'm not in a position to keep you in therapy and I obviously respect your wishes.

CLIENT: I know you've been rather pessimistic about the progress I've made, but I feel I've made sufficient progress to warrant my return to work and no more sessions.

THERAPIST: It certainly isn't my job to quell enthusiasm. It's more my job to create enthusiasm, but I must admit I'm not at all happy about this because I can see all kinds of problems cropping up and at this point, I don't think you are going to be able to handle them. In fact, I would predict that you couldn't.

CLIENT: Oh! What kind of problems are these?

THERAPIST: Well, I can see problems at work for a start. Now that you're better, you are going to be expected to pull your weight to the full—you'll be in at the deep end—as soon as you go back to work. At home, your family is going to expect you to behave and function the way you used to before the problem started. I just think that's too big a task at the moment.

CLIENT: I'm sure I could do it.

THERAPIST: Well, I wonder if you could. Help me out, because I'm not happy with this. I know you feel you don't need any further sessions, but just to ease my conscience, would it be OK if I did three follow-ups at 1-monthly intervals? These wouldn't be full sessions, but would just give me the opportunity to see how you're getting on and you could let me know if any of the problems I've indicated are actually occurring.

If the client accepts this, he has the therapist's challenge of imminent failure and he must therefore work harder at being successful. From the client's point of view, the therapist has offered three follow-up visits for her own, totally selfish, reasons. From the therapist's point of view, not only have the prediction and challenge of failure been given, but she has also negotiated three further sessions. Although defined as follow-up sessions, in terms of monitoring progress, they can actually be used by the therapist to impart implicit information. She is also able to re-enforce, either negatively or positively, the client's response to the challenge of imminent failure.

Sometimes termination of treatment by the client is arrived at unwillingly. This may be due to circumstances, for example, moving out of the area, or by duress from other family members. Perhaps the rationale for moving house to a different area is to 'start afresh' or geographical escape. However, the move to another area could also be perfectly genuine, due to change of employment. In either case, the therapist has the opportunity to grant discharge at short notice, but with sufficient time to implement various strategies which should help to prevent relapse. For example:

THERAPIST: Your wish to terminate these sessions is rather sudden. I wonder if you could let me know what's happening?

CLIENT: We have to move out of this area as I have the offer of another job. Anyway, we've both decided to make a fresh start away from this place, which is where all our problems began.

THERAPIST: I'm certainly glad to hear about the job, but I'm not so sure about your other reason for moving. It seems to me that perhaps you are being a little unrealistic. The trouble with problems is that they are not geographical; they tend to follow you around in your head. I can remember when I moved house to my current job, I had a bad shoulder. All the time I was actually moving house and sorting out the new house I didn't even feel the pain. About 3 days later, once the new house was sorted out, all of a sudden the pain was back.

CLIENT: I know what you mean, but it won't be like that for us. We have decided to bury the past and start afresh.

THERAPIST: That's an interesting statement—'bury the past'— where are you going to bury it—in the back garden—on the beach? Where?

CLIENT: I don't know what you mean. We're just going to forget about the past.

THERAPIST: Unfortunately the past is always there in your mind. It may not be at the front of your mind and it may not even be at the back of your mind, but it is locked in there. There is no way you can erase previous experiences or previous memories. I'm sorry to be pedantic about this but it seems to me that you are doing yourself a disfavour—not because you are moving, but because of the Utopian ideas you seem to have about the move. You seem to think that if you move, then everything from the past will stay in the old house and I'm afraid that is just not so. I would prefer it if you at least accept that the past comes with you in your own mind and that you are prepared to adopt some techniques which will diminish the influence of the past on present-day behaviours or relationships.

CLIENT: I'm not sure I'm with you.

THERAPIST: Well, let me put it this way. I predict that within 3 months you will begin to find yourself getting back into a similar situation. I also predict that you may remember this conversation and begin to get frustrated and angry. When this happens, quite often common sense flies out of the window. As soon as you get angry, I reckon you will fall into the same patterns as you are in just now. Not only that, but with exactly the same results. That is, you and your wife will not talk to each other, you will begin to drink, your performance at work will deteriorate, your wife will get even more upset and anxious, and so on. Her way of expressing her anxiety will be to nag you, which will continue the vicious circle.

CLIENT: I'm sure it won't happen like that.

THERAPIST: I certainly hope it doesn't ... I can see the potential for it happening. What I would like you to do when this happens is to sit down with your wife and just say: 'You are perfectly right—let's sort it out together'.

In this example, not only has the therapist delivered the predicted challenge, she has also included what has, until now, never happened in terms of successful marital interaction. If the predicted relapse occurs, not only has the therapist been proven right, but the client will realise that she has also predicted a possible way out of such marital conflict.

In a situation where the client undergoes therapy in every successive area he moves to, again predictions of relapse or failure can be given. Also, where appropriate, in terms of the 'professional patient', a sense of success can be transmitted. For example:

CLIENT: I haven't been able to get any help here, so I'm going to another area.

THERAPIST: I am sorry and disappointed that we haven't made any tangible progress here, but I said at the beginning of therapy that I wouldn't be surprised if we did not make any progress.

CLIENT: What do you mean by that? I don't remember you saying that.

THERAPIST: I'm sure I did—I think. I can't remember when, but I thought I actually did say that I was impressed by the number of therapists you had seen previously. Not only that, but I know that these are some of the best therapists around. I reckoned that if they couldn't help you, I was pretty sure I would be unable to help you. Thinking about it, I honestly can't remember whether I said it or not, but I know I certainly thought it.

In this instance, the therapist has indicated disappointment at the lack of progress and in this case of the 'professional patient' who does not generally respond, the client is given the enjoyment of the therapist's impotence. He is also given the challenge that if he enters into therapy in a different area, it is predicted that therapy will fail. If the client takes the challenge up, the only way to thwart this therapist's prediction is to prove her wrong; when he next enters therapy it must be successful.

The preceding examples are situations when the client terminates treatment; when this occurs it is usually to the surprise of the therapist, despite signs and symptoms possibly being evident during previous sessions. The above techniques and strategies are therefore merely thumb-nail sketches to give some idea of the positions the therapist can use to make the best of what is possibly a bad situation.

The other way that treatment is terminated is by the therapist herself. By definition, this should be more controlled, less un-expected and, using certain skills and techniques, the therapeutic outcome should be much more successful. Termination of therapy in this instance should not be seen as a special significant event, but rather the continuing process of the client re-achieving functional levels.

In the more lengthy models of therapy, there is the opportunity for 'special' relationships (that is, transference) to develop between the client and therapist. In these instances, consideration must be given not only to the need for discharge, but also to the impact on the relationship. However, this eclectic model believes that therapy should be as fast and as painless as possible. As such, there is less possibility of a 'special' relationship developing and therefore less need to summarise the achievements which have been accomplished within therapy. This approach is geared more towards resolving specific problems. Therefore, dealing with discharge or termination of treatment should be equally brief. 'The goal of treatment, generally, is to eliminate or sufficiently reduce the complaint so that the client will not feel that further treatment is necessary, at least for the the original complaint, and termination is the logical step after the complaint has been resolved' (Fisch *et al.*, 1982).

Using these criteria, the main problems are ensuring continued functioning following termination of therapy and the possibility that, when faced with discharge, the client will respond in such a way as to make sure that treatment continues. For example:

THERAPIST: It seems to me that we have now successfully achieved the goals we initially set out when you originally defined your problem.

CLIENT: Yes, I know that we've reached these goals, but there is something else which bothers me as well and I thought perhaps we could look at that now.

THERAPIST: Is this a problem that came up during the course of sorting this problem out, or is it one that has always been there?

CLIENT: I guess it has always been there.

THERAPIST: This problem was not sufficiently severe earlier on when we started, otherwise I assume you would have mentioned it. Are you saying that since beginning treatment for the existing problem, another problem which you didn't know about has actually increased in intensity?

In this instance, the client is faced with the decision of whether or not this problem was pre-existing at the time of initiating therapy. As stated by the therapist, if it was pre-existing, then it was not of sufficient importance at that time for the client to mention it to the therapist. If, however, the client states that this problem has increased in intensity since commencing this course of therapy, the client is responsible for not indicating the problem earlier, especially if in previous sessions the therapist has indicated the 'danger of improvement', that is, as one problem is resolved, another may take its place. However, the therapist is faced with the dilemma that the client is seeking to maintain therapeutic contact with her and she must judge whether or not continued involvement is advisable, on the merits of each individual case. If the therapist considers continued contact is advisable, then she must make out another treatment programme with separate goals to be achieved. If, on the other hand, the therapist believes that the emerging problem does not warrant further sessions, then there is still the problem of disengagement and discharge.

Some clients will indicate that although they have received what they expected from therapy and to the level they had hoped, they still feel nervous and anxious about stopping treatment. Others, on the other hand, will agree that it is time to stop and will indicate little anxiety related to discharge. 'It is the safer assumption that most clients will feel some uncertainty that the accomplishments of treatment will sustain themselves once treatment is over, and some patients will be quite explicit about that' (Fisch *et al.*, 1982). If the therapist is aware of and appreciates this fact, then the process of discharge should be made easier. However, the client's anxiety regarding cessation of treatment may be sufficient for him to try harder to keep things the way they were. In this way, the client may unwittingly bring on the spontaneous paradox and as a result, fail in the continuance of functioning, that is, he may re-commence dysfunctioning.

One method of relaxing the client's perception of possible relapse is the 'go slow' intervention, which is defined in *The Tactics of Change* (Fisch *et al.*, 1982) as follows: 'The therapist will begin by acknowledging that improvement has occurred but will then interject the comment that, desirable as the change is, it has occurred too fast.' By requesting the client to 'go slow', the therapist is asking him not to make any further effort to improve things. This can be defined as a temporary measure to allow the transition from treatment to non-treatment and also to make the foundation of the treatment experience more solid.

As a word of warning, it is unwise for the therapist to congratulate the client on discharge with such praise as: 'You've done really well. I'm really pleased for you.' This will highlight any possible recurrence of symptoms or relapse, since it will be thought that the therapist has gauged the situation wrongly. If this is the case and the client is re-referred to treatment, then the therapist has diminished her own position. It is much wiser to terminate treatment with such statements as: 'I hope things will turn out all right for you.' In this case the therapist can defend her situation by stating: 'Well, I wasn't too sure that you would actually succeed anyway.'

The aforementioned are all methods of using certain skills and techniques when faced with the decision of termination of treatment. However, this alone does not help the therapist decide when treatment should be terminated. If she uses the contract number of sessions approach to therapy and the client or therapist decides to terminate treatment with sessions still outstanding, then these sessions can be held in abeyance and used in the future at the client's request. If, on the other hand, the agreed contracted number of sessions has reached its limit, then the therapist should review the situation with the client and decide what factors are preventing progress, either on the part of the client or, more importantly, on the part of the therapist. Once a client has reached the allocated number of sessions, there is no reason why a re-negotiated contract of further sessions should not take place. However, this is not a prescription for continued unlimited treatment but should only take place after intense, careful analysis of why therapy is not working. If these factors can be identified, then the therapist should accept them and alter the therapeutic approach accordingly. This can quite easily be done with the simple statement: 'It seems to me that in the last group of sessions, I have actually misunderstood what you have been saying and what has been happening. I would therefore like to start afresh and perhaps you could tell me what the problem is now.' This is not only a re-opening of negotiations on further treatment, but is also an immediate re-enforcement of the therapist's 'one-down' position.

The logical answer to the question: 'When should therapy stop?' is 'When the client has achieved and accepted achievement

Termination Sheet

Client /Family name .... Date ....

Number of sessions .... Date of first session ....

Reason for termination

Therapist: Client:

Original goal

Amended goals(s) if any and date

Major interventions during treatment and dates

Results of treatment

Final intervention

Therapist ....

Fig. 8.1   *Termination sheet*

of his goals as originally set out'. Problems can occur however when the client fails to agree with the therapist that he has reached his goals. A situation can quickly develop whereby 'more of the same' interaction takes place; the more the therapist states that the client has achieved his goals, the more the client will say that his problems have not really changed. This discussion results in prolonged therapy and also probably creates an acrimonious atmosphere, which is obviously not conducive to therapy.

On termination of treatment it is useful to have a factual account of the progress of treatment on one sheet of paper (Fig. 8.1). It is useful to know the number of sessions which have taken place over what period of time. Under the heading 'Reason for termination' the therapist can insert in her section such statements as: 'geographical move'; 'goals achieved'; 'goals partially achieved', or even 'client dissatisfaction'. The same reasons are applicable to the client and the client's statements should be recorded honestly if any benefit is to be gained from the learning experience of assessing the therapist's performance. In the clinic-based setting, it is advisable if the person interviewing the client regarding the reason for termination is not the front therapist. This is to minimise the possibility that the client will give polite and perhaps untrue reasons for terminating treatment, due to the relationship built up between client and therapist during the sessions. Under the heading 'Original goal' should be recorded the negotiated original goals at the outset of therapy. Under the heading 'Amended goal(s) if any' would come revised goals if the therapist or the client realised during the process of treatment that perhaps the original goals were out of reach. This could also include new goals set in cases when the original goals were achieved extremely rapidly and the need for on-going therapy outweighed the need for discharge at that time, hence the need for revised goals to have the dates of amendment recorded. Under 'Major interventions during treatment and dates' should be listed interventions which, in the view of the therapist, greatly influenced and accelerated the process whereby the client or family regained functional control. This information may prove useful at a later date if the client re-encounters difficulties. 'Results of treatment' should include the shifts in interactions or communications which now indicate how or to what extent the original problem has been minimised or completely eradicated. 'Final intervention' should indicate what the therapist leaves the client or family with. For example, it is advised that at the termination of any therapy contract, the therapist should leave the family with a statement designed to hinder relapse or at least to imply that if relapse occurs, then the client does have control over this, either in terms of what he has learned from the therapy sessions or in terms of spontaneous paradox. It would be policy discretion whether or not this sheet should be circulated to referral sources and/or other professionals involved. This has advantages and disadvantages.

If this sheet is completed on termination of therapy and inserted into the client's file and the family is re-referred at a later date, any therapist who takes up the case can see at a glance all the necessary information regarding which methods or interventions were most successful and how fast the client or family is liable to respond. This can cut down the length of time in treatment and should allow the therapist, if required, to re-negotiate the conditions required for entry into therapy.

The level of activity during therapy can be likened to flights to the moon. The level of activity at NASA headquarters increased at certain points during the flight. Activity increased during the period from countdown to blast-off. As the spacecraft left Earth's atmosphere, tension was relieved and a lower level of activity took place. When the spacecraft was due to enter the moon's orbit, activity increased again, as it did when the spacecraft was out of communication contact on the opposite side of the moon. The next high level of activity was the departure from the moon's orbit back to Earth. So it is with therapy. Following the high level of activity of taking in information, assessing, evaluating and setting the client tasks, the therapist can relax a little and await the client's response. If the client's response is that he is in correct 'orbit', the therapist knows the client is on the right path. This does not mean that having found the right path, the client will remain on it. There are therefore several points where high levels of activity and vigilance are required. However, once the client is on the 'homeward journey', the therapist has the option of remaining with the client until 'splash-down' is achieved or she can disengage herself from the process. Disengagement is based on the theory that if the spacecraft is pointing toward Earth and has sufficient momentum to reach Earth, barring re-entry problems, there should be a safe 'splash-down'. It is not necessary for the therapist to remain in therapy with the client once it becomes evident that there is a momentum of previous achievements and a momentum of a particular method of functioning.

One of the main problems related to discharge is human curiosity. An example of human curiosity is if, when telling a child the fairy tale of Cinderella, you end the story at the point where the prince orders all women in the land to try on the glass slipper. The conclusion of the story can be deduced because it is known that the glass slipper will only fit one foot and if all women have to try it on, then obviously it will only fit Cinderella's foot. However, it is impossible to stop the story at the point where logical deduction tells you the ending, as the child will nevertheless demand to hear the end of the story. Likewise with therapy; one hears such statements as: 'I want to see the family one more time, just to make sure they are OK' or 'There is a big transition coming up and I want to see them safely through it'. These are examples of human curiosity and the need for the therapist to remain in therapy until she achieves her own goals. If the therapist has created the right atmosphere and given the client the right direction, once he shows movement toward success, the momentum of that movement will achieve satisfactory therapeutic results.

It is not uncommon to hear staff at community agencies making the statement: 'I am a bit slack just now, so I have to hold on to all the clients I have; otherwise my boss will wonder what I'm doing.' Nor is it uncommon to hear the statement: 'I've done my best—let them get on with it.' These statements are indicative of the level of empathy exhibited by the therapist toward the client or family and as such, do not hold much hope for the therapeutic process.

In an earlier example, follow-up was used as a means of continuing therapy sessions, albeit indirectly. If the therapist feels some anxiety regarding the release of a client, the option of follow-up can be used and there is no harm in pursuing this avenue to the client's benefit. If the therapist does employ this strategy, then the sessions should be follow-up sessions and not therapy sessions. She should be aware that they are for her benefit in this instance and not for the client's benefit and the less involvement there is, the better.

As Philip Barker stated (1986): 'It is not usually a good idea for us as therapists to take credit for the changes families make, however clever we may think we are.' For example, a colleague once informed me of his experience when he employed family therapy skills and techniques for the first time, with astounding success. On discharging the families, he contacted the referring agencies, in this case their GPs, and stated that he felt he had done 'a wonderful job' and the skills and techniques he had used were obviously the reason for this drastic improvement. Then certain GPs suddenly stopped referring to him. Within a short space of time, it became apparent that the referrals were drying up from the surgeries where he had indicated his part in the success. Realising his mistake, he returned to the surgeries and stated that he had been over-zealous in stressing his own importance and on reflection, looking through the medical records, he thought the transformation in the families was probably due to a change of medication by the GP or the result of some unconscious dynamic interaction which had taken place during the client's last visit to the GP. He was amazed that the 'dried up' referral sources suddenly started referring again. The moral of this factual account is that at no point should the therapist take any credit whatsoever for any progress made. If the therapist takes the credit, by implication, the other professionals who are or were involved have been unsuccessful and have been using the wrong approach. Despite our professional attitudes, it is hard for any human being to take the criticism, whether implicit or explicit, that he has failed in his methods of trying to help.

Discharge of the Walker family, discussed in previous chapters, took place as follows:

THERAPIST: I can't keep up with all these new things you are trying as a family. I'm getting more and more confused, so I would suggest that for the time being, I don't actually see you again.

MRS WALKER: You can't do that. You can't leave us high and dry. I know we've done well and things are getting better, but we still need you.

THERAPIST: I don't see how you need me. It's you as a group who are making all the advances and it's me who is getting left behind. If anything, I need you to help me.

MRS WALKER: By the way, what was it you did that initially got us on the road to where we are?

THERAPIST: I didn't do anything other than give you some

advice. I didn't actually do anything. I'm not on the road you are on, so there is no way I can be responsible for you being on that road.

MRS WALKER: I've heard of this family therapy and I've read one or two things about it. I think that somewhere along the line, you tricked us into getting better.

THERAPIST: Are you insinuating that I would stoop so low as to use underhand tricks to get you better?

MRS WALKER: I'm sorry. I didn't mean to offend you. I didn't really mean that.

THERAPIST: If you didn't really mean it, then why did you say it? I think you actually meant it and I'm somewhat pleased that you think I had some part to play in you getting over your problems ... I am flattered. But, I honestly don't see that I've done anything for you, other than be there.

During the several months following the Walker family's discharge from treatment, the therapist received telephone calls from Mrs Walker, who said: 'Now that we are officially off the books, you can tell us what these tricks were.' The therapist replied: 'I'm pleased that you are getting on well, but I really do feel hurt that you think I would use tricks.' This pattern of telephone conversations continued for approximately 3 months and then ceased completely.

For those who are interested in the story rather than therapeutic progress, the result of the Walker family story was that Mrs Walker was seen by the therapist some years later in an antenatal clinic. During conversation, Mrs Walker told the therapist that she was there for the supervision of her fifth pregnancy. (Mrs Walker was originally referred because of non-accidental injury of her eldest child and at that time, presented with extreme sexual problems. She did not enjoy or desire sexual intercourse and in fact had ceased physical sexual contact for a period of some months.) The therapist replied:

THERAPIST: You seem to have got over your sex problem then?

MRS WALKER: Not only is sex more enjoyable now—I also enjoy the children. In fact, instead of criticising the way I bring up my children, my GP now holds me up as an example of how someone can cope and get over what appear to be insurmountable problems.

Discharge should be the ultimate goal of treatment and should be: 'Discharged—cured. This phrase should not mean "Let's keep our fingers crossed"' (MacPhail, 1983).

Summary

This chapter highlighted the need for controlled and planned discharge. Examples were given of how to minimise relapse by challenge, prediction and prescription. The timing of discharge was also discussed.

Discharge need not only take place when all goals are satisfactorily achieved, but also when the client is moving in the correct direction at sufficient momentum.

The need for a discharge/termination sheet was explained and its usefulness outlined.

The therapist was encouraged, as at all times during therapy, to evaluate her own position as well as that of the client.

Exercises

1 Who is requesting discharge? Client or therapist?
2 How many goals have been achieved or how close is the client to achieving them?
3 Do you try to prevent relapse when discharging clients? Try using prediction or prescription the next time.
4 Go through your case load and identify how many are re-referrals to you or your service. (Then look at the terms or conditions of previous discharge.)
5 Check your discharge letters for the kind of information a new therapist would need. Compare with Fig. 8.1.
6 Check whether the client needs to continue in therapy. (Whose needs are being catered for—client or therapist?)

References

MacPhail, W. D. (1986). Skills in family therapy. *Nursing Times*; 82: 26: 51.

Fisch, R., Weakland, J. H., Segal, L. (1982). *The Tactics of Change*. London, Jossey-Bass, pp. 175–83.

Barker, P. (1986). *Basic Family Therapy*, 2nd edn. London, Collins, p. 247.

MacPhail, W. D. (1983). Brief therapy. *Nursing Times*; 157: 11: 38.

9

Evaluation

This chapter will look at the evaluation of the success of this model of therapy in terms of some of the problems not mentioned previously.

Evaluation of the Success of Therapy

It can be very difficult for the therapist to evaluate the outcome of therapy, as various options are open to the client on termination of treatment. If therapy is successful, the client does not need to seek help elsewhere. However, if therapy is only partially successful or is totally unsuccessful, the client has the option of returning to his GP, who may himself counsel the client or refer him to a different agency. The GP may also refer the client to a different service out of the area or even to a private service. It is therefore difficult for the therapist to ascertain whether or not the client has been referred on. Depending on the therapist's relationship with the GP, it may be possible for her to check the GP's records to assess how many times and for what reasons the client has approached the GP for advice since the discharge date. It may also be possible to discover the outcome of any counselling undertaken by the GP.

Some community psychiatric nursing services advocate personal follow-up of discharged clients. This can either take the form of visiting the client at home or inviting him to return to the service base for a follow-up interview. It is also possible for services to use a postal follow-up sheet (Fig. 9.1).

As discussed in Chapter 8, it is more beneficial in terms of gaining objective information if the follow-up interviewer is not the identified therapist in previous treatment. If a particular therapist attempts to elicit information regarding her own performance, there are obviously various reasons why the client may tend to exaggerate or hide his responses.

Outcome of Treatment

Dear ....

Some 3 months ago you were discharged from treatment by the community
psychiatric nurse. In order to improve the type and quality of service we offer,
I would be grateful if you could complete the questionnaire below and return it
to me in the envelope provided.

Please tear off the section below if you wish to retain anonymity.

....

1 Have you experienced any recurrence of your original symptoms?

   No [ ]   A little [ ]   Some [ ]   A lot [ ]

2 Have you experienced any new symptoms?

   No [ ]   A little [ ]   Some [ ]   A lot [ ]

3 Have you experienced any new problems?

                 Yes [ ]   No [ ]

4 Are you able to manage these new problems?

   Well [ ]   Partially [ ]   Poorly [ ]

5 Have you sought professional advice since last seeing the CPN?

                 Yes [ ]   No [ ]

Thank you for your co-operation.

Yours sincerely

Community Psychiatric Nurse

Fig. 9.1 *Postal follow-up of outcome of treatment*

There are basically five questions which need to be asked to identify the outcome of therapy:

1 'Has there been any recurrence of the original symptoms?' The response to this question indicates how successful therapy was in dealing with the original presenting problem and related symptoms.
2 'Has the client experienced any new symptoms?' The response to this question indicates any progression from previous symptoms to new, different symptoms. This could mean that therapy was only partially successful in alleviating previous symptoms, since symptoms still occur, although of a different nature.
3 'Has the client experienced any new problems or transitions?' This would indicate any new symptoms related to any new problems. Irrespective of the success of previous therapy for a particular problem, the client will obviously encounter further problems in life. It is hoped that an awareness of and ability to overcome problems has been activated in the client during therapy and that any new problems will have minimal impact in terms of functioning or, at least, will not lead to the intensity or levels of dysfunction previously experienced.
4 'Evaluate whether or not the client is better able to manage any new problems.' As previously outlined, new symptoms and new problems may have arisen which do not necessarily lead to dysfunction as hopefully the client has learned methods during therapy which will help him.
5 'Has the client sought professional advice regarding any new problems or symptoms since termination of treatment?' It is possible that, although any new problems may be relatively intense, the client's perception is that he is able to handle them. If, however, he has sought professional advice elsewhere, via the GP to other community agencies or to psychotherapy, he may be indicating some dissatisfaction with the previous treatment sessions. If, for whatever reason, the client has sought further treatment elsewhere, the therapist should re-examine the case, preferably with a colleague. The clinic-based therapist is in a better position for observation by colleagues, who may well have acted as co-therapists during the treatment sessions. Also, if video equipment is available to the clinic-based therapist, it may be possible to re-run the relevant video

recordings of the treatment sessions and attempt to identify the point at which an interaction or request caused the client to become dissatisfied.

From experience, it seems that the most common time for evaluation to take place is approximately 3 months, 6 months and 1 year following termination of treatment. This is however by no means rigid and no doubt each individual service has its own optimum timespan for evaluation.

It cannot be over-emphasised that the most important aspect of evaluating the outcome of treatment is the learning process for the therapist. Some therapists contend that the surest method of evaluation is physical evaluation. By being physically present, the therapist is able to assess, evaluate and see at first hand whether or not the skills the family have learned in therapy are in fact being utilised. The interactions and relationships within the family are visible and the therapist therefore has a truer picture of the success of previous sessions.

Evaluation of therapy, especially in situations where there are colleagues to assist, is not only invaluable as a learning experience for the therapist, it is also an ideal opportunity for training other family therapists. This training should include didactic and theoretical learning as well as experiential learning. As Freisen (1985) states: 'There is an interaction between talent and training. That is, we cannot become family therapists as a result of talent or training alone.' This is therefore an opportune moment to incorporate the training of family therapists by exposure to the evaluation process, which will also provide theoretical and audiovisual re-enforcement to the skills and techniques employed. It is essential that the trainee initially receives this orientation to family therapy prior to attempting a live interview. Once induction to family therapy has been completed, the trainee can progress to live sessions with identified supervisors. This process can be facilitated for the clinic-based family therapist by the use of one-way screens or video recordings. However, in community-based set-ups, co-therapy has to be provided by the supervisor's physical presence in the room. It is perhaps easier to learn and more constructive during these sessions if the supervisor designates a relevant period of time, for example 5 or 10 minutes, when the trainee can be advised of his progress and if necessary, re-directed on to a slightly different path. These sessions can however cause problems for the supervisor who is supervising not only the trainee, but also the interaction and flow of therapy between trainee and the family. If the supervisor does not maintain some form of balance between these two functions there can be constant irritating interruptions, causing the process of therapy to become very disjointed and the family, and possibly the trainee, to be distracted.

At present there are courses run by or accredited by the English National Board for community psychiatric nurses and for the supervision of community psychiatric nurses, but not solely in family therapy. However, until standardised courses on family therapy become available for both trainee therapists and therapists, training must be undertaken by therapists who are already practising to a satisfactory level.

There are no time limits on the duration of any particular stage of training family therapists. It seems that the most integrated method of training is a system in which theoretical training is given for several hours per week, interspersed with observation of video tapes of previous sessions to highlight the theoretical points, and involvement in the observation of live therapy sessions. Following the satisfactory conclusion of this stage of training, the trainee would then become the front therapist under supervision. As Haley (1976) states: 'Ideally he (the therapist) learns to do therapy by doing it while guided by a supervisor at the moment therapy is happening.'

However, although extremely important in the organisation of community psychiatric nursing services, training alone may actually prove detrimental to the individual growth of the therapist as: 'It is a sign of a mature and well trained professional who realises that he or she has limitations, and that good practice involves having consultations available and using them when necessary' (Barker, 1986). If such training programmes become available, it is extremely important that each individual community psychiatric nursing service should send more than one of its members on the course. It can be very demoralising for the therapist to have a problem within any model of family therapy and be unable to turn to anybody for advice or support.

There are of course, existing courses in family therapy run by organisations or individual hospitals. However, in the present climate of restricted spending, it is improbable and in some cases, impossible for community psychiatric nurses to be seconded on to these courses, which tend to be either day-release over a period of years or block-release over a period of weeks or months, when the cost tends to be prohibitive. Nonetheless, it is imperative that community psychiatric nurses should be trained in family therapy as it would be potentially dangerous for an untrained therapist to practise in this field. There is therefore a need for nationally organised courses in each health authority or the inclusion of family therapy into the basic RMN training or, more selectively, into the training of community psychiatric nurses. However, we do not live in a Utopian society where everything which is needed ideally is provided and community agencies must therefore make the most of what is available.

Evaluation of this Model of Therapy

As mentioned at the beginning of this chapter, there are some areas of psychiatry which have not been included so far, either as theory or as examples. Due to their relatively common-place existence within psychiatry, these areas will now be briefly discussed. There are also other skills and techniques which have not yet been mentioned and these too will be described.

Anorexia and bulimia

Anorexia and bulimia are both disorders in which there are disturbed eating patterns. In anorexia there is generally a desire or compulsion not to eat to achieve or maintain a specific body weight or body image. In bulimia the same principle of body weight and body image applies, but this syndrome is characterised by bingeing (eating large amounts of food), usually followed by purging (the emission of such food from the body system either by enforced vomiting or purgatives).

There are many theories regarding the psychodynamic causation of these problems. One theory is of relationship problems as in the 'mother–daughter relationship' or the 'disturbed father–daughter relationship' (Freisen, 1985). Another theory is: 'A poor boundary structure between individuals and between generations' (Freisen, 1985). It is also suggested that: 'These families emphasise the themes of closeness, avoidance of conflict at all costs, unrealistic expectations, no separate emotional existence and the inability to tolerate sexuality' (Freisen, 1985). A more common theory exists that: 'A female anorexic is in a competitive relationship with her mother' (Freisen, 1985). Irrespective of the theories of causation of anorexia or bulimia, most theorists believe that: 'she (the anorexic) becomes a very central and powerful influence in the family'. As in other problems encountered by clients in psychiatry, there is the belief—which is expressed by the client—that the client is unable to control or stop this pattern of behaviour. As Vognsen (1985) states: 'As food must be mastered several times a day, it is especially important in treating eating disorders that the client comes to see herself as responsible for her cure.'

It may be interesting to know the cause of the onset of such eating disorders, but in this model of therapy the cause if relatively unimportant. It is more constructive for the problem to be seen as being maintained by the attempted solutions used to try and control the behaviour. The process of bulimia, as described by Vognsen (1985), is an almost accidental initial encounter with bingeing and purging and a secondary realisation that there is a connection between eating and body weight. Vognsen states that most bulimics will deliberately binge and purge in such a way as to meet: 'Unusual circumstances such as a feast or a period of loneliness and critical self-examination.' He states that there is a transition from deliberate conscious manipulation of this process to secrecy and a conscious denial of the process. He states: 'The bulimic cheats in the pursuit of pleasure and the perfect body and denial and secrecy mask the fraudulent manner in which she achieves the feat of eating her cake and keeping her shape as well.' The secrecy of anorexia and bulimia is regarded as the beginning of the lacking-control process. As described earlier in this eclectic model, the foremost task of the therapist should be to block the attempted solutions. An initial task could be to ask the client to keep a diary of how often she eats, what she eats and where food is eaten. This begins to counteract the aspect of secrecy. By not insisting that these behaviours should cease, the therapist is undermining the thread of compulsion and non-control which weaves its way through the process. This is later accelerated, for example, by asking the client to have both planned and spontaneous binges. These requests can be justified as the need to gather data more precisely or specifically. This alone may lead to a reduction in or even a complete cessation of the problematic behaviour.

For this client, the 'go slow' theory may also be applied; she is asked to slow down the rate of change from bingeing and purging to normality. This can be implemented by asking the client to binge periodically and consciously and can be deemed to be a prescription of the symptom. As such, any form of relapse is controlled and prescribed and not uncontrollable, as earlier described. To prevent a habitual relapse, the therapist can set tasks, which the client is expected to perform when an unacceptable level of relapse occurs, with the intention of making it easier and more productive for the client to avoid the task, rather than relapse back into the problem. For example, if the previous pattern of problematic or ill behaviour re-emerges, the therapist can ask the client to set her alarm clock for 2 o'clock in the morning and get up at this time. The client should then either perform a task which is unpleasant to her or just write down the events of the previous day. This can be justified by saying that people are generally more relaxed and able to think clearly at that time of the morning.

The medical aspects of anorexia and bulimia must be considered and it is therefore generally unwise to prescribe or ask the client to continue purging, as this may lead to intestinal problems. In this instance, the focus of the problem should be on the binging as, if binging does not occur, there is no need for purging to follow. It is also best if interventions are: 'Directed at the patient's eating problem and framed to the patient as information seeking tasks rather than treatment' (Moley, 1983).

Another method of dealing with these clients is pattern intervention. As previously described (p. 179), this entails interrupting the pattern in which the client is able to pursue the process. For example, the therapist could ask the client to wear her best dress or best shoes when purging. This is sometimes sufficient to prevent purging taking place. Another method of pattern intervention would be to request the client to liquidise all food to be binged prior to ingestion.

It is essential for follow-up to take place in the treatment of eating disorders. As eating is something people have to do every day to maintain existence, the possibility of relapse is therefore greater. However, an anecdote in Vin Moley's paper (1983) regarding the client's perception of treatment is given below:

THERAPIST: Have any new problems developed?

CLIENT: I am having to deal with success which I have never had to. That's even scarier than failure.

Vin Moley goes on to say: 'This brings to mind John Weakland's aphorism to the effect that: "When you have a problem, life is the same damn thing over and over again: when you are over the problem, life is just one damn thing after another".'

Phobias and obsessions

In terms of re-framing and making therapy easier, it is useful to use the term 'anxiety states'. Phobias are, by definition, an anxiety state and obsessions and compulsions can be deemed to be rituals or methods employed in order to avoid an anxiety state. Therefore, the former is a pure anxiety state and the latter an avoidance. With all anxiety states, it is essential to maintain a realistic outlook on the goals to be achieved. It is very common for anxious clients to see as their goal the complete cessation of all anxiety symptoms. However, in terms of normalisation, this is unrealistic. As with eating disorders, anxiety states have a common theme in that the attempted solutions to the problem often make resolution impossible. It should therefore be the therapist's aim to stop the attempted solutions and, if nothing else at that point, to allow the clients to formulate solutions to their own problems.

There are various methods of dealing with anxiety states: behavioural, psychoanalytical and interactional approaches, to name but three. In his attempted solution, the client will try to prepare for the anxiety-provoking situation 'By attempting to master it in advance' (MacPhail and McMillan, 1983). From experience, the approach which seems to be the most effective is that of intervening in the pattern of behaviour or interaction immediately preceding the anxious state. The client who experiences anxiety in certain situations usually states that his anxiety is aroused at the mere mention of the feared situation. Once his anxiety is aroused, he will attempt to fight it by focussing on it and trying to reassure himself that the fear is illogical. However, this process focuses even more attention and concentration on the feared situation. This, in turn, will initiate the physical symptoms associated with anxiety, such as: increased breathing rate—when the client becomes conscious of this, he associates it with physical inability to face or tolerate the situation; palpitations—which can lead the client to believe there is some physiological reason for the anxiety, such as heart attack; symptoms of tension in various muscles—stomach, legs, chest, shoulders or neck. As this process continues, the client will become more anxious and at some point, the anxiety will focus away from the feared situation to anxiety regarding his physical health. The following is an extract from a recent session:

THERAPIST: Could you tell me what the problem is?'

CLIENT: Well, I don't understand it. I don't like going on trains. When I go on trains, I get panics. But that's only part of the problem. The other part is because of stress at work, I think I might be heading for a heart attack.

THERAPIST: Could you tell me which occurred first, the uneasiness regarding travelling on trains or the fear of a heart attack?

CLIENT: The fear of going on trains came first. I just wasn't able to travel long distances on the train and because I commute to London, the situation at work has become intolerable.

THERAPIST: Could you tell me how this relates to what you describe as your fear of having a heart attack?

CLIENT: Well, it all started on the train one day when, because I was getting into a panic, I suddenly started having chest pains and palpitations. At the same time I felt the blood rush to my head and I went hot and cold.

THERAPIST: Do you see these two things as separate, consecutive or actually one and the same?

CLIENT: I think there probably is a connection, but it seems to me that because of my work, I am heading for a heart attack.

From this conversation it can be seen how easily the physical sensations overtake the client and are sometimes seen as separate from the anxiety symptoms. Once the therapist has established the pattern of physical symptoms, that is the order in which they occur, she can either present the client with tasks or alter the pattern. For example:

THERAPIST: Could you tell me exactly what happens to you when these panics occur and if possible, in what order?

CLIENT: First of all, for no apparent reason, I suddenly find that my heart is beating faster and as I become aware of that, I start to breathe faster. Then I feel hot and cold and sweaty and as this progresses, I feel I must escape from wherever I am.

THERAPIST: How long does this entire process take?

CLIENT: It feels like a quarter of an hour but it's probably only a few minutes.

THERAPIST: What I would like you to do is—by the way, do you wear shoes with laces in them?

CLIENT: Yes, I do.

THERAPIST: Then what I would like you to do is, when you believe the faster breathing is about to start, bend over and undo the lace on your left shoe and then do it back up again and then stand or sit back up. Then I want you to bend down again and undo and do up the lace on the other shoe.

If the client follows this simple task, the effect is that by physically bending over, it will be impossible for hyperventilation to take place because of the contraction of the diaphragm and other muscles associated with the chest. This is a good example of the theory that the client does not have to understand the causation of the problem in order to stop it. Once the client is aware that these symptoms are controllable, then the symptoms will come under control and fade or disappear completely.

The same principle applies to obsessional behaviour. The client can be asked to re-arrange the pattern of the obsession in such a way that the symptoms or the conscious awareness of the symptoms are unattainable. For example, in the case of obsessional hand-washing, having found out the specific behaviours which make up the pattern, the therapist can ask the client, the next time he goes to the toilet, to hold the soap in the opposite hand to usual and to wash the hands a specific number of times, rather than for a generalised time limit:

THERAPIST: I would like you to wash your hands—each hand 14 times.

Another example of changing the pattern of behaviour would be in the case of a woman who obsessionally and ritualistically cleans the house with each room being on a priority list. She can be advised to alter the priority list. For example:

THERAPIST: It seems to me that you are very particular and efficient in the methods you use to clean your house. However it does seem that you are actually making a lot of unnecessary work for yourself. I would suggest that instead of starting your cleaning routine downstairs, you start upstairs. It seems a bit unwise starting downstairs when the family is still there as you have to clean round them and as soon as they have gone, you then have to re-clean these areas anyway. I would also suggest that rather than starting with your own bedroom, you start in the children's bedroom as this is probably by far the most untidy. Once you have done that room, you can reassure yourself that the rest gets easier.

By altering the pattern in this way, the client can no longer continue being ritualistic and if the advice is undertaken, the pattern is broken anyway.

The use of metaphor in family therapy 'Offers many possibilities for the indirect communication of ideas and for strategic intervention in families' (Barker, 1986). Metaphors allow the therapist to make indirect allusion to the client of what she considers to be an important interaction or important relationship. For example, if an important family member is missing from a session:

THERAPIST: Where's John today?
MOTHER: He couldn't come.
THERAPIST TO SON: Was it something I said?
MOTHER: I don't think so.
THERAPIST TO DAUGHTER: Was it something I did?

The metaphor is that all family members present should identify with this and ask themselves the same questions and therefore look at their own role within the family interaction.

Barker (1985) lists seven classifications of therapeutic metaphors:

1 Major stories designed to deal comprehensively with complex clinical situations.
2 Anecdotes and short stories aimed at achieving specific limited goals.
3 Analogies, similes and brief metaphorical statements or phrases that illustrate or emphasise specific points.

4 Relationship metaphors.
5 Tasks with metaphorical meanings.
6 Metaphorical objects: as an example of this, Barker describes the use of an envelope containing a blank sheet of paper to represent a family secret.
7 Artistic metaphors—these are artistic productions such as drawings, paintings, clay models or structures built with Lego which are used to represent a feeling, state, experience or something else which may be significant in the treatment process.

It can be seen from this list that metaphors can be particularly useful when, for example, therapy becomes stuck or when there is an evident need to avoid direct confrontational communication. The use of metaphor enhances the non-confrontational approach without detracting from the message or experience the therapist wishes to impart.

Lastly, there is the technique of hypnosis, which, despite the myths surrounding it, is becoming more and more prevalent within the range of techniques employed by family therapists. The mystique surrounding hypnosis is perhaps understandable because most people's experience of hypnosis is that presented by the media, that is, theatrical hypnosis, as opposed to hypnosis used in clinical settings. Hypnosis can best be defined as an altered state of consciousness. The hypnotic trance, on the other hand, is a specific process or procedure which involves deep relaxation and the freeing of the mind to enable the acceptance of suggestions. An example of altered state of consciousness could be the driver who suddenly finds himself 2 miles further along the route than he thought he was and who cannot remember passing certain landmarks of which he would normally be aware. Another example could be suddenly finding yourself in a room, looking for something, but not remembering having passed through other rooms to get there. Altered levels of consciousness are therefore quite common and are the basis of trance. Light trances can be readily achieved in clients.

Zahourek (1985) itemises several possible purposes for the use of hypnosis and hypnotic techniques in psychotherapy as follows:

• Reducing anxiety and stress.

- Exploring possibilities when confronted with difficult decisions.
- Altering psychosomatic symptoms.
- Removing unwanted habits.
- Building transference and a positive therapeutic relationship.
- Regressing to past traumatic events for catharsis and re-structuring.
- Eliminating blocks in the therapeutic process.
- Controlling unwanted thoughts or perseverations.
- Understanding unconscious processes.

Obviously the use of hypnosis for deep trance states requires specific training and it is not the purpose of this book to enter into that depth, but rather to look at the possibilities of light trance within the therapeutic session. The therapist can use imagery as a means to relax the client as follows:

THERAPIST: I would like you to shut your eyes and visualise what you would call a relaxing scene or situation. Without interrupting the process of visualising that scene, I would like you to tell me about it. First of all start by describing what is in the foreground and then work your way to the background. Try and include as much detail as you can possibly give me.

As the client progresses with the visualisation, the therapist can ask for greater detail as the description unfolds. It is sometimes quite useful to extend the imagery through the appropriate senses. For example:

THERAPIST: You have told me the scene is a beach. Can you tell me the colour of the sand? Or is it pebbles? Can you tell me what sound the sea is making? Is it the sound of big waves or little waves hitting the beach? Can you describe the smell of the sea? Can you see any vegetation in the scene? Can you describe it to me?

Each of these questions asks the client to broaden his perceptual senses and thus enter deeper into the trance. As the involvement and imagery go deeper, the therapist can note the change in the client's rhythm of breathing which will become slower and he will begin to look more relaxed. By asking the client how relaxed he is on a scale of 0–10, the therapist can judge whether or not to make suggestions. The more relaxed the client is, the more accepting he will be of the suggestion. Zahourek (1985) states that: 'Suggestions might be made subtly' such as: 'Just as you solved a problem last week, so you can solve this current one.'

Having relaxed the client by imagery or by relaxation tapes, it is important for the therapist to utilise the sensation of deep relaxation. The client can be asked to focus on one specific part of his body, for example, a finger. The therapist can then suggest that the feeling of relaxation can be recalled post-trance just by focusing on that particular finger. This is a useful technique for anxiety and stress reduction.

This process is also useful in the management of disruptive or aggressive clients. For example:

THERAPIST: I am here to help you but I am finding it difficult to do so as long as you remain so tense. I would like you to take a deep breath, come with me across the room and sit down in that chair. As you relax you will find that you are more in control and able to relax even more. Once you are relaxed, then we can try and sort out what the problem is.

If this message is repeated in the correct quiet, soft tone of voice, while imparting empathy, the client will respond by becoming less tense and as a result, less aggressive or agitated.

There is certainly a place for hypnosis in psychiatric nursing, but the therapist should be trained in the process and procedures before attempting hypnosis.

'An often overlooked source of invaluable skill is the therapist and her life experience. All too often, the therapist feels that she should not reveal too much of her own values, priorities, beliefs or perceptions as she may then lose control. But the empathetic response is invaluable in developing a relationship based on mutual experience and emotion.

'These skills do not come easily or fluently but need practice and more practice until they become second nature. Then and only then with change in the perception of the illness process, does therapy become what it should be, enjoyable and fun' (MacPhail, 1986).

Summary

The need for evaluation and follow-up was highlighted in this chapter. The various methods—physical, postal or via the GP—were mentioned, as was the desirability of having colleague support in evaluation.

Methods of training therapists were given and the necessity of training more than one person per team at a time was emphasised. The problems of such training, namely financial restrictions, were also mentioned, as was the need for a centralised national training programme run by an organisation such as the English National Board or further education departments.

Some categories of problems not dealt with previously were highlighted, namely anorexia, bulimia, phobia and obsession, as well as therapy approaches to these problems.

The skills and techniques of metaphor usage and hypnosis were exemplified, especially the potential of hypnotic techniques. However, it was stressed that nurses must be trained in all the techniques set out in this book if they are to be effective.

Exercises

1 Do you already do some form of formalised follow-up or evaluation? If so, what do you do with the information gained, both statistically and therapeutically?
2 If no formalised evaluation or follow-up takes place, how do you know how efficient you are?
3 All nurses or therapists should check their case loads. How many re-referrals do you or your service get? What percentage is that? Is it acceptable?
4 Do you train new staff in your therapeutic skills? How do you evaluate this?
5 Compare how relaxed and tense clients respond to your suggestions or requests.
6 Do you enjoy your work? If not, which areas are unpleasant and what will you do about them?
   (Try re-framing them.)

References

Barker, P. (1985). *Using Metaphors in Psychotherapy*. New York, Mazel.

Barker, P. (1986). *Basic Family Therapy*. London, Collins.

Freisen, P. D. (1985). *Structural–Strategic Marriage and Family Therapy*. London, Gardner Press.

Haley, J. (1976). *Problem Solving Therapy*. New York, Harper Colophon Books, p. 181.

MacPhail, W. D. (1986). Skills and family therapy. *Nursing Times*; 82:26:51.

MacPhail, W. D., McMillan, I. (1983). Fighting phobias. *Nursing Mirror*; 157:7:ii.

Moley, V. (1983). Interactional treatment of eating disorders. *Journal of Strategic and Systemic Therapies*; 2.

Vognsen, J. (1985). Brief strategic treatment of bulimia. *Transactional Analysis Journal*, 15: 79–84.

Zahourek, R. P. (1985). *Clinical Hypnosis and Therapeutic Suggestion in Nursing*. London, Grune & Stratton, pp. 225–44.

Further Reading

O'Hanlon, W. H., Wilk, J. (1987). *Shifting Contexts: The Generation of Effective Therapy*. Guildford Press, New York.

Index